180 DELICIOUS VEGETARIAN
POTATO RECIPES

180 DELICIOUS VEGETARIAN
POTATO RECIPES

MOUTHWATERING MEAT-FREE RECIPES THAT FEATURE THE WORLD'S
BEST-LOVED VEGETABLE, ILLUSTRATED IN 200 STUNNING PHOTOGRAPHS

Elizabeth Woodland

southwater

This edition is published by Southwater,
an imprint of Anness Publishing Ltd,
Blaby Road, Wigston, Leicestershire LE18 4SE
Email: info@anness.com

www.southwaterbooks.com;
www.annesspublishing.com

If you like the images in this book and would like to investigate
using them for publishing, promotions or advertising, please visit
our website www.practicalpictures.com for more information.

Publisher: Joanna Lorenz
Project Editor: Daniel Hurst
Jacket Design: Lesley Mitchell
Production Controller: Bessie Bai

PUBLISHER'S NOTE
Although the advice and information in this book are believed to
be accurate and true at the time of going to press, neither the
authors nor the publisher can accept any legal responsibility or
liability for any errors or omissions that may have been made nor
for any inaccuracies nor for any loss, harm or injury that comes
about from following instructions or advice in this book.

© Anness Publishing Ltd 2011

ETHICAL TRADING POLICY
At Anness Publishing we believe that business should be conducted in
an ethical and ecologically sustainable way, with respect for the
environment and a proper regard to the replacement of the natural
resources we employ. As a publisher, we use a lot of wood pulp to
make high-quality paper for printing, and that wood commonly comes
from spruce trees. We are therefore currently growing more than
750,000 trees in three Scottish forest plantations: Berrymoss (130
hectares/320 acres), West Touxhill (125 hectares/305 acres) and
Deveron Forest (75 hectares/185 acres). The forests we manage
contain more than 3.5 times the number of trees employed each
year in making paper for the books we manufacture.
Because of this ongoing ecological investment programme, you,
as our customer, can have the pleasure and reassurance of knowing
that a tree is being cultivated on your behalf to
naturally replace the materials used to make the book you are
holding. Our forestry programme is run in accordance with
the UK Woodland Assurance Scheme (UKWAS) and will be certified
by the internationally recognized Forest Stewardship Council (FSC).
The FSC is a non-government organization dedicated to promoting
responsible management of the world's forests. Certification ensures
forests are managed in an environmentally sustainable and socially
responsible way. For further information about this scheme, go to
www.annesspublishing.com/trees

Previously published as part of a larger volume, *500 Potato Recipes*

Notes

Bracketed terms are intended for American readers.

For all recipes, quantities are given in both metric and imperial measures and, where appropriate, in standard cups and spoons.
Follow one set of measures, but not a mixture, because they are not interchangeable.

Standard spoon and cup measures are level. 1 tsp = 5ml, 1 tbsp = 15ml, 1 cup = 250ml/8fl oz. Australian standard tablespoons
are 20ml. Australian readers should use 3 tsp in place of 1 tbsp for measuring small quantities.

American pints are 16fl oz/2 cups. American readers should use 20fl oz/2.5 cups in place of 1 pint when measuring liquids.
Electric oven temperatures in this book are for conventional ovens. When using a fan oven, the temperature will probably need to
be reduced by about 10–20°C/20–40°F. Since ovens vary, you should check with your manufacturer's instruction book for guidance.
The nutritional analysis given for each recipe is calculated per portion (i.e. serving or item), unless otherwise stated.
If the recipe gives a range, such as Serves 4–6, then the nutritional analysis will be for the smaller portion size, i.e. 6 servings.
Measurements for sodium do not include salt added to taste. Medium (US large) eggs are used unless otherwise stated.

Main front cover image shows Baked Scalloped Potatoes with Feta – for recipe see page 39.

Contents

Introduction

There are few more important foods in the world than the potato. Its history goes back to the early days of man and it has long played a vital role as one of the best all-round sources of nutrition for mankind.

The potato was discovered by pre-Inca inhabitants in the foothills of the Andes Mountains in South America. Archaeological remains have been found dating from 400BC on the shores of Lake Titicaca, in ruins near Bolivia, and on the coast of Peru.

The first recorded information about the potato was written in 1553 by the Spanish conquistador Pedro Cieza de Leon, and soon potatoes joined the treasures carried away by Spanish invaders. Its cultivation spread quickly throughout Europe via explorers such as Sir Francis Drake, who is reputed to have brought potatoes back to Britain. During Charles II's reign, the Royal Society recognized the potato as being nutritional and inexpensive and tried to persuade their farmers to start growing this valuable crop in abundance.

The United States, one of the world's largest producers of potatoes, was introduced to the potato by early European immigrants, but it was not until the Irish took the potato to Londonderry, New Hampshire, in 1719, that it began to be grown there in any quantity.

Today the potato is the staple food for two-thirds of the world's population and our third most important food crop. Growing potatoes is also the world's most efficient means of converting land, water and labour into an edible product – a field of potatoes produces more energy per acre per day than a field of any other crop. It is one of the best complete sources of nutrition known to man, which makes it an essential component of the vegetarian diet.

This book explores the infinite adaptability of the potato in meat-free cooking and is the ultimate resource for the potato-loving vegetarian cook. As you'd expect, it includes all the classic potato dishes, such as Potato and Leek Vichyssoise, Shepherdess Pie and Vegetarian Moussaka, but we've also investigated every conceivable way of introducing our favourite ingredient into some familiar and much-loved dishes. There are delicious and deceptively easy Gruyère and Potato Soufflés, a hearty and warming Grated Potato Casserole, an exotic and delicately spiced Potato Curry with Yogurt and a decadent and festive Sweet Potato Pie.

Other tempting and surprising recipes include a flavoursome Jerusalem Artichoke and Potato Rösti, an impressive Vegetable Gratin with Indian Spices, and a delightfully piquant Goan Potato Soup with Samosas. There are distinctive variations of classic potato dishes as well as a seemingly endless array of new and exciting recipes that will be sure to broaden your potato repertoire and have you cooking delectable meat-free potato dishes every day of the week.

The recipes are split into six easy-to-use sections which divide the book between Soups; Appetizers and Snacks; Salads; Main Courses; Side Dishes; and finally Desserts, Bakes and Breads, making it easy to find the perfect potato dish, whatever the occasion. Whether you are looking for a sensational potato recipe for a formal dinner party, a simple and nutritious dish for a mid-week family meal, or a light and tasty snack to keep you going through the afternoon, the plethora of wonderful potato recipes on display here will be sure to deliver the perfect dish time and time again.

This book is the ultimate celebration of an underrated staple of the vegetable kingdom and clearly illustrates the many delicious uses of the potato, whatever the variety – whether you are using large maincrop potatoes, small new potatoes or candied sweet potatoes. Expand your culinary horizons and unlock the potential of the nutritional powerhouse of the vegetable world, the humble potato, today.

Potato and Leek Vichyssoise

This classic, chilled potato soup was first created in the 1920s by Louis Diat, chef at the New York Ritz-Carlton. He named it after Vichy, near his home in France.

Serves 4–6

50g/2oz/¼ cup unsalted (sweet) butter
450g/1lb leeks, white parts only, thinly sliced
3 large shallots, sliced
250g/9oz floury potatoes (such as King Edward or Maris Piper), peeled and cut into chunks
1 litre/1¾ pints/4 cups vegetable stock or water
300ml/½ pint/1¼ cups double (heavy) cream
iced water (optional)
a little lemon juice (optional)
salt and ground black pepper
chopped fresh chives, to garnish

1 Melt the butter in a heavy pan and cook the leeks and shallots gently, covered, for about 15–20 minutes, until soft but not browned.

2 Add the potatoes and cook, uncovered, for a few minutes. Stir in the stock or water with 5ml/1 tsp salt and pepper to taste. Bring to the boil, then reduce the heat and partly cover the pan. Simmer for 15 minutes, or until the potatoes are soft.

3 Cool, then process the mixture until smooth in a blender or food processor. Strain the soup into a bowl and stir in the cream. Taste and adjust the seasoning and add a little iced water if the consistency of the soup seems too thick.

4 Chill the soup for at least 4 hours or until very cold. Before serving, taste the chilled soup for seasoning and add a squeeze of lemon juice, if required. Pour the soup into bowls and sprinkle with chopped chives. Serve immediately.

Variation
Add about 50g/2oz/1 cup shredded sorrel to the soup at the end of cooking. Finish and chill as in the main recipe, then serve the soup garnished with a little pile of finely shredded sorrel. The same quantity of watercress can be used in the same way.

Spicy Chilled Cardamom, Leek and Potato Soup

This subtly spiced version of the classic potato vichyssoise is enhanced with fragrant cardamom and topped with the refreshing tang of yogurt.

Serves 4

8 green cardamom pods
25g/1oz/2 tbsp butter
15ml/1 tbsp vegetable oil
1 small onion, chopped
3 leeks, sliced
2 floury potatoes, diced
600ml/1 pint/2½ cups vegetable stock
300ml/½ pint/1¼ cups milk
45ml/3 tbsp single (light) cream
a little extra milk (optional)
grated zest of 1 small lemon
60ml/4 tbsp natural (plain) yogurt and fried leeks, to serve
salt and ground black pepper

1 Scrape out the seeds from the cardamom pods and grind them to a fine powder in a mortar and pestle.

2 Heat the butter and oil in a large pan and add the onion, leeks, ground cardamom and potatoes. Cover and cook for 15 minutes, stirring occasionally, until the leeks have wilted and given up their juices. Bring to the boil, reduce the heat to a gentle simmer and cook for 10 minutes.

3 Stir in the stock and milk and heat until simmering. Cover again and cook for a further 15 minutes, until the vegetables are completely tender.

4 Ladle the vegetables and liquid into a blender or a food processor in batches and purée until smooth. Pour into a bowl or jug (pitcher) for chilling. Stir in the cream and grated lemon zest and season.

5 Leave the soup to cool, and then refrigerate for 3–4 hours, or longer until chilled and ready to serve. You may need to add a little extra milk to thin down the soup, as it will thicken up slightly as it cools.

6 Ladle the soup into soup bowls and serve topped with a spoonful of natural yogurt and a sprinkling of leeks.

Vichyssoise Energy 547kcal/2260kJ; Protein 4.6g; Carbohydrate 17.7g, of which sugars 6.8g; Fat 51.4g, of which saturates 31.7g; Cholesterol 129mg; Calcium 79mg; Fibre 3.6g; Sodium 103mg.
Spicy Cardamom Energy 410kcal/1695kJ; Protein 3.5g; Carbohydrate 13.2g, of which sugars 5.1g; Fat 38.5g, of which saturates 23.8g; Cholesterol 97mg; Calcium 59mg; Fibre 2.7g; Sodium 77mg.

Creamy Leek, Potato and Rocket Soup

Rocket adds its distinctive, peppery taste to this wonderfully creamy potato and leek soup. Serve this soup hot, garnished with a generous sprinkling of tasty ciabatta croûtons flavoured with garlic.

Serves 4–6
50g/2oz/¼ cup butter
1 onion, chopped
3 leeks, chopped

2 medium floury potatoes, diced
900ml/1½ pints/3¾ cups
   vegetable stock or water
2 large handfuls rocket (arugula),
   roughly chopped
150ml/¼ pint/⅔ cup double
   (heavy) cream
salt and ground black pepper
garlic-flavoured ciabatta croûtons,
   to garnish

1 Melt the butter in a large heavy pan, then add the chopped onion, leeks and diced potatoes and stir until the vegetables are coated in butter. Heat until the ingredients are sizzling, then reduce the heat to low.

2 Cover and sweat the vegetables for 15 minutes. Pour in the chicken stock or water and bring to the boil. Reduce the heat, cover again and simmer for about 20 minutes until all the vegetables are tender.

3 Press the soup through a sieve (strainer) using a wooden spoon, or pass it through a food mill, and return the mixture to the rinsed-out pan. (When puréeing the soup, don't use a blender or food processor, as these will cause the soup to develop a gluey texture.)

4 Add the chopped rocket to the pan and continue to cook the soup gently, uncovered, for 5 minutes.

5 Stir in the double cream, then season to taste with salt and black pepper and reheat gently. Ladle the soup into warmed soup bowls and serve with a sprinkling of garlic-flavoured ciabatta croûtons in each.

Chunky Leek, Onion and Potato Soup

The nutritious combination of leek, onion and potato makes for a really tasty and substantial soup. It is incredibly simple to make and the ingredients are fresh, inexpensive and readily available to buy throughout the year, which makes this an essential addition to any home cook's repertoire.

Serves 4
50g/2oz/¼ cup butter
2 leeks, chopped
1 small onion, finely chopped
350g/12oz floury
   potatoes, chopped
900ml/1½ pints/3¾ cups
   vegetable stock
salt and ground black pepper
crusty bread, to serve

1 Heat 25g/1oz/2 tbsp of the butter in a large heavy pan, add the chopped leeks and onion and cook gently, stirring occasionally so that they do not stick to the bottom of the pan. Cook for about 6–8 minutes until the vegetables have softened but not browned.

2 Add the chopped potatoes to the pan and cook, stirring occasionally, for 2–3 minutes.

3 Pour in the stock and slowly bring to the boil, then reduce the heat, cover and simmer gently for 30–35 minutes until the vegetables are cooked through and very tender.

4 Season to taste with salt and black pepper, remove the pan from the heat and stir in the remaining butter in small pieces.

5 Ladle the soup into warmed soup bowls and serve hot with slices of thick crusty bread.

Cook's Tip
If you prefer your soup to have a smoother consistency, simply press the mixture through a sieve (strainer) or pass through a food mill once it is cooked. Don't use a food processor as it can give the potatoes a gluey texture.

Creamy Leek Soup Energy 235kcal/972kJ; Protein 2.8g; Carbohydrate 9.4g, of which sugars 3.2g; Fat 20.9g, of which saturates 12.8g; Cholesterol 52mg; Calcium 75mg; Fibre 2.3g; Sodium 97mg.
Chunky Leek Soup Energy 178kcal/744kJ; Protein 3.4g; Carbohydrate 17.8g, of which sugars 3.9g; Fat 11.1g, of which saturates 7g; Cholesterol 29mg; Calcium 33mg; Fibre 3g; Sodium 288mg.

Creamed Spinach and Potato Soup

This is a delicious low-fat potato soup that is both quick and simple to make. This recipe uses spinach but other vegetables would work just as well, such as cabbage or Swiss chard.

Serves 4
1.2 litres/2 pints/5 cups
    vegetable stock
1 large onion, finely chopped
1 garlic clove, crushed

900g/2lb floury potatoes, diced
2 celery sticks, chopped
250g/9oz fresh spinach leaves
200g/7oz/scant 1 cup low-fat
    soft (farmer's) cheese
300ml/½ pint/1¼ cups milk
dash of dry sherry
salt and ground black pepper

For the garnish
croûtons
a few baby spinach leaves or
    chopped fresh parsley

1 Place the stock, onion, garlic, potatoes and celery in a large pan. Bring to the boil, reduce the heat and cover the pan. Simmer the soup for 20 minutes.

2 Season the soup and add the spinach leaves, then bring back to the boil. Reduce the heat to a gentle simmer and cook for a further 10 minutes. Remove from the heat and cool slightly.

3 Process the soup in a food processor or blender until smooth and return it to the rinsed-out pan.

4 Stir in the soft cheese and milk. Reheat gently without boiling and taste for seasoning. Add a dash of sherry.

5 Ladle the soup into bowls and serve topped with croûtons and a few baby spinach leaves or chopped fresh parsley.

Cook's Tip
A hand-held blender is excellent for quickly puréeing soups in the pan. Remove the pan from the heat and let it cool slighlty first. Take care to keep the blender well down in the pan, otherwise the soup will spray everywhere. Start on a low setting to break up some of the ingredients, then increase the speed.

Summer Herb Soup with Potato

The sweetness of shallots and leeks in this soup is balanced beautifully by the potatoes and slightly acidic sorrel, with its hint of lemon, and a bouquet of summer herbs.

Serves 4–6
30ml/2 tbsp dry white wine
2 shallots, finely chopped
1 garlic clove, crushed
2 leeks, sliced
1 potato, about 225g/8oz,
    roughly chopped

2 courgettes (zucchini), chopped
600ml/1 pint/2½ cups
    boiling water
115g/4oz sorrel, torn
large handful of fresh chervil
large handful of fresh flat
    leaf parsley
large handful of fresh mint
1 round or butterhead lettuce,
    separated into leaves
600ml/1 pint/2½ cups
    vegetable stock
1 small head radicchio
5ml/1 tsp groundnut (peanut) oil
salt and ground black pepper

1 Put the wine, shallots and garlic into a heavy pan and bring to the boil. Cook for 2–3 minutes, until softened. Add the leeks, potato and courgette with enough of the water to come about halfway up the vegetables. Lay a wetted piece of baking parchment over the vegetables and put a lid on the pan, then cook gently for 10–15 minutes, until softened. Remove the paper and add the fresh herbs and lettuce. Cook for 1–2 minutes, or until wilted.

2 Pour in the remaining water and vegetable stock and simmer for 10–12 minutes. Cool the soup slightly, then process it in a food processor or blender until smooth. Return the soup to the rinsed-out pan and season well.

3 Cut the radicchio into thin wedges that hold together, then brush the cut sides with the oil. Heat a ridged griddle or frying pan until very hot and add the radicchio wedges. Cook the radicchio wedges for about 1 minute on each side until very well browned and slightly charred in places.

4 Reheat the soup over a low heat, stirring occasionally, then ladle it into warmed shallow bowls. Serve a wedge of charred radicchio on top of each portion.

Creamed Spinach Soup Energy 274kcal/1157kJ; Protein 15.3g; Carbohydrate 46.2g, of which sugars 11.6g; Fat 5g, of which saturates 2.7g; Cholesterol 13mg; Calcium 281mg; Fibre 4.4g; Sodium 348mg.
Summer Herb Energy 199kcal/837kJ; Protein 10.2g; Carbohydrate 29.2g, of which sugars 12.6g; Fat 4.4g, of which saturates 0.9g; Cholesterol 0mg; Calcium 227mg; Fibre 8.6g; Sodium 94mg.

Potato and Fennel Soup

This light potato and fennel soup is delicious served with moreish rosemary scones.

Serves 4
75g/3oz/6 tbsp butter
2 onions, chopped
5ml/1 tsp fennel seeds, crushed
3 bulbs fennel, coarsely chopped
900g/2lb potatoes, thinly sliced
1.2 litres/2 pints/5 cups
   vegetable stock
150ml/¼ pint/⅔ cup double
   (heavy) cream

salt and ground black pepper
handful of fresh herb flowers and
   15ml/1 tbsp chopped fresh
   chives, to garnish

For the rosemary scones
225g/8oz/2 cups self-raising
   (self-rising) flour
2.5ml/½ tsp salt
5ml/1 tsp baking powder
10ml/2 tsp chopped fresh rosemary
50g/2oz/¼ cup butter
150ml/¼ pint/⅔ cup milk
1 egg, beaten, to glaze

1 Melt the butter in a pan. Add the onions and cook gently for 10 minutes, stirring occasionally, until very soft. Add the fennel seeds and cook for 2–3 minutes. Stir in the fennel and potatoes. Cover with wet baking parchment. Cover and simmer gently for 10 minutes, until very soft. Remove the parchment. Pour in the stock, bring to the boil, cover and simmer for 35 minutes.

2 Meanwhile, make the scones. Preheat the oven to 230°C/450°F/Gas 8 and grease a baking tray. Sift the flour, salt and baking powder into a bowl. Stir in the rosemary, then rub in the butter. Add the milk and mix to form a soft dough.

3 Knead very lightly on a floured surface. Roll out to 2cm/¾in thick. Stamp out 12 rounds with a cutter and place on the baking tray. Brush with egg and bake for 8–10 minutes, until risen and golden. Cool on a wire rack until warm.

4 Purée the soup in a food processor or blender until smooth. Press through a sieve (strainer) into the rinsed-out pan. Stir in the cream with seasoning to taste. Reheat gently but do not boil.

5 Ladle the soup into bowls, and sprinkle over a few herb flowers and some chopped chives. Serve with the warm rosemary scones.

Broad Bean and Potato Soup

Coriander provides a refreshing twist to this creamy soup of fresh beans and hearty potatoes.

Serves 4
30ml/2 tbsp olive oil
2 onions, chopped
3 large floury
   potatoes, diced

450g/1lb fresh shelled broad
   (fava) beans
1.75 litres/3 pints/7½ cups
   vegetable stock
1 bunch fresh coriander (cilantro),
   roughly chopped
150ml/¼ pint/⅔ cup single
   (light) cream, plus a little extra,
   to garnish
salt and ground black pepper

1 Heat the oil in a large pan and fry the onions, stirring, for about 5 minutes, until they are soft.

2 Add the potatoes. Reserve a few of the broad beans for garnish, then add the rest to the pan. Pour over the stock, and bring it to the boil. Simmer the soup for 5 minutes, then add the coriander and simmer for a further 10 minutes.

3 Blend the soup in batches in a food processor or blender until smooth, then return it to the rinsed-out pan.

4 Reheat the soup until almost boiling, stirring to prevent it from sticking to the pan. Stir in the cream and heat for a few seconds, but do not allow the soup to simmer or boil.

5 Blanch the reserved beans in boiling water for 1 minute, then drain them and remove their skins.

6 Taste and season the soup, then ladle it into bowls and garnish with beans, cream and chopped coriander.

Variation
Instead of the broad (fava) beans, try a combination of peas – shelled fresh or frozen – and a bunch of watercress in this recipe. The peas and watercress are delicious with the coriander (cilantro).

Potato and Fennel Energy 797kcal/3332kJ; Protein 12.3g; Carbohydrate 84.1g, of which sugars 8.8g; Fat 48.1g, of which saturates 29.6g; Cholesterol 120mg; Calcium 316mg; Fibre 7.6g; Sodium 703mg.
Broad Bean and Potato Energy 236kcal/990kJ; Protein 9.3g; Carbohydrate 30.3g, of which sugars 4.6g; Fat 9.4g, of which saturates 3.8g; Cholesterol 14mg; Calcium 94mg; Fibre 6.8g; Sodium 30mg.

Spinach and Root Vegetable Soup

This is a slow-cooker version of a typical Russian soup, which is traditionally prepared when the first vegetables of spring appear. You will need to use a large slow cooker in order to accommodate the spinach.

Serves 4

1 small turnip, cut into chunks
2 carrots, diced
1 small parsnip, cut into large dice
1 potato, peeled and diced
1 onion, chopped

1 garlic clove, finely chopped
¼ celeriac bulb, diced
750ml/1¼ pints/3 cups boiling vegetable stock
175g/6oz fresh spinach, roughly chopped
1 small bunch fresh dill, chopped
salt and ground black pepper

For the garnish

2 hard-boiled eggs, sliced lengthways
1 lemon, sliced
30ml/2 tbsp fresh parsley and dill

1 Put the turnip, carrots, parsnip, potato, onion, garlic, celeriac and vegetable or chicken stock into the ceramic cooking pot of the slow cooker.

2 Set the cooker to the high or auto setting and cook for 1 hour, then either leave on auto or switch to low and cook for a further 5–6 hours, until the vegetables are soft and tender.

3 Stir the spinach into the cooking pot and cook on high for 45 minutes, or until the spinach is tender but still green and leafy. Season with salt and pepper.

4 Stir in the dill, then ladle the soup into warmed bowls and serve garnished with egg, lemon slices and a sprinkling of fresh parsley and dill.

Cook's Tip
For best results, use a really good-quality vegetable stock in this soup – either home-made or bought fresh from a delicatessen or supermarket.

Roast Vegetable Medley

Winter meets summer in this soup recipe for chunky roasted vegetables. Serve it with bread baked with a hint of added summer flavour in the form of sun-dried tomatoes.

Serves 4

4 parsnips, quartered lengthways
2 red onions, cut into thin wedges
4 carrots, thickly sliced
2 leeks, thickly sliced
1 small swede (rutabaga), cut into chunks
4 potatoes, cut into chunks
60ml/4 tbsp olive oil

few sprigs of fresh thyme
1 bulb garlic, broken into cloves, unpeeled
1 litre/1¾ pints/4 cups vegetable stock
salt and ground black pepper
fresh thyme sprigs, to garnish

For the sun-dried tomato bread

1 ciabatta loaf
75g/3oz/6 tbsp butter, softened
1 garlic clove, crushed
4 sun-dried tomatoes, finely chopped
30ml/2 tbsp chopped fresh parsley

1 Preheat the oven to 200°C/400°F/Gas 6. Cut the thick ends of the parsnip quarters into four, then place them in a large roasting pan. Add the onions, carrots, leeks, swede and potatoes, and spread them in an even layer.

2 Drizzle the olive oil over the vegetables. Add the thyme and unpeeled garlic cloves. Toss well and roast for 45 minutes, until all the vegetables are tender and slightly charred.

3 To make the sun-dried tomato bread, slice the loaf without cutting right through. Mix the butter, garlic, sun-dried tomatoes and parsley. Spread the butter between the slices. Wrap in foil. Bake for 15 minutes, opening the foil for the last 4–5 minutes.

4 Discard the thyme from the vegetables. Squeeze the garlic from its skins over the vegetables and purée half the mixture with the stock. Pour into a pan. Add the remaining vegetables. Bring to the boil and season well.

5 Ladle the soup into bowls and garnish with fresh thyme leaves. Serve the hot bread with the soup.

Spinach Soup Energy 229kcal/952kJ; Protein 7.8g; Carbohydrate 14.3g, of which sugars 9.2g; Fat 16.2g, of which saturates 8.7g; Cholesterol 133mg; Calcium 197mg; Fibre 4.1g; Sodium 148mg.
Vegetable Medley Energy 511kcal/2146kJ; Protein 13.9g; Carbohydrate 72.6g, of which sugars 18.9g; Fat 20.4g, of which saturates 10.6g; Cholesterol 40mg; Calcium 218mg; Fibre 12.1g; Sodium 521mg.

Potato and Spring Onion Soup

The sumptuously spring onion flavour of this creamy chilled soup is surprisingly delicate, thanks to the potatoes, quantity of stock and the addition of tangy lemon juice.

Serves 4–6
25g/1oz/2 tbsp butter
1 small onion, chopped
150g/5oz/1¾ cups spring onions (scallions), chopped

225g/8oz potatoes, peeled and chopped
600ml/1 pint/2½ cups vegetable stock
350ml/12fl oz/1½ cups single (light) cream
30ml/2 tbsp freshly squeezed lemon juice
salt and ground white pepper
chopped spring onions (scallions) or fresh chives, to garnish

1 Melt the butter in a pan and add all the onions. Cover and cook over a very low heat for about 10 minutes or until soft.

2 Add the potatoes and the stock. Bring to the boil, then cover the pan again and simmer over a moderately low heat for about 30 minutes. Cool slightly.

3 Purée the soup until smooth in a food processor or blender.

4 If serving the soup hot, pour it back into the pan. Add the cream and season with salt and pepper. Reheat gently, stirring occasionally. Add the lemon juice.

5 If serving the soup cold, pour it into a bowl. Stir in the cream and lemon juice and season with salt and pepper. Cover the bowl and cool, then chill for at least 1 hour.

6 Serve sprinkled with the chopped spring onions or chives.

> **Variation**
> *For a lighter version that is still satisfyingly creamy, use olive oil instead of butter and plain (natural) yogurt instead of cream and omit the lemon juice.*

Pasta-free Potato Minestrone

Minestrone is the famous Italian soup that can be made with almost any combination of seasonal vegetables. Many recipes are bulked out with pasta, but the combination of vegetables used here and the addition of pesto ensures that the soup is both substantial and flavoursome.

Serves 6
1.75 litres/3 pints/7½ cups vegetable stock
1 large onion, chopped

3 celery sticks, chopped
2 carrots, finely diced
2 large floury potatoes, finely diced
½ head of cabbage, very finely diced
225g/8oz runner (green) beans, sliced diagonally
2 x 400g/14oz cans cannellini beans, drained
60ml/4 tbsp ready-made pesto sauce
salt and ground freshly ground black pepper
crusty bread, to serve
freshly grated Parmesan cheese, to serve

1 Pour the stock into a large pan. Add the onion, celery and carrots. Bring to the boil, reduce the heat and cover the pan. Then simmer for 10 minutes.

2 Add the potatoes, cabbage and beans to the soup and simmer for 10–12 minutes or until the potatoes are tender.

3 Stir in the cannellini beans and pesto, and bring the soup to the boil, stirring frequently.

4 Season the soup to taste and serve hot, with crusty bread and plenty of freshly grated Parmesan cheese for adding to individual portions as required.

> **Variation**
> *This already substantial soup can be made a real feast by adding a handful of either rice or barley with the vegetables in step 1 above. Instead of floury potatoes, dice small, waxy salad potatoes that will hold their shape and stay firm but tender during cooking to complement the grains.*

Spring Onion Soup Energy 179kcal/744kJ; Protein 3.2g; Carbohydrate 8.9g, of which sugars 3.1g; Fat 14.8g, of which saturates 9.3g; Cholesterol 41mg; Calcium 67mg; Fibre 0.9g; Sodium 48mg.
Pasta-free Minestrone Energy 241kcal/1007kJ; Protein 9.7g; Carbohydrate 21.7g, of which sugars 9.3g; Fat 13.4g, of which saturates 4g; Cholesterol 13mg; Calcium 204mg; Fibre 3.6g; Sodium 165mg.

Spicy Potato and Red Lentil Soup

Red lentils and vegetables are cooked and puréed, then sharpened with lots of lemon juice. In hot weather, this soup is also good served cold, adding even more lemon. It is also known as 'Esau's soup' and it is sometimes served as part of a Sabbath meal in Jewish households.

Serves 4
45ml/3 tbsp olive oil
1 onion, chopped
2 celery sticks, chopped
1–2 carrots, sliced
8 garlic cloves, chopped
1 potato, peeled and diced
250g/9oz/generous 1 cup
    red lentils
1 litre/1³⁄₄ pints/4 cups
    vegetable stock
2 bay leaves
1–2 lemons, halved
2.5ml/¹⁄₂ tsp ground cumin, or
    to taste
cayenne pepper or Tabasco sauce,
    to taste
salt and ground black pepper
lemon slices and chopped
    fresh flat leaf parsley leaves,
    to serve

1 Heat the oil in a large pan. Add the onion and cook for about 5 minutes, or until softened. Stir in the celery, carrots, half the garlic and all the potato. Cook for a few minutes until beginning to soften.

2 Add the lentils and stock to the pan and slowly bring to the boil. Reduce the heat, cover and simmer for about 30 minutes, until the potato and lentils are tender.

3 Add the bay leaves, remaining garlic and half the lemons to the pan and cook the soup for a further 10 minutes. Remove the bay leaves. Squeeze the juice from the remaining lemons, then stir into the soup, to taste.

4 Pour the soup into a food processor or blender and process until smooth. (You may need to do this in batches.) Transfer the soup back into the pan and heat through, stir in the cumin, cayenne pepper or Tabasco sauce, and season.

5 Ladle the soup into warmed bowls and top each portion with lemon slices and a sprinkling of chopped fresh flat leaf parsley.

Chunky Potato, Split Pea, Mushroom and Barley Soup

This hearty vegetable soup from Eastern Europe is perfect on a freezing cold day. Serve it in warmed bowls, with plenty of rye (pumpernickel) bread. This is a vegetarian version that is bulked out with slow-cooked pulses and potatoes. For a meat version, use meat stock instead of vegetable and add chunks of tender, long-simmered beef to the soup.

Serves 6–8
30–45ml/2–3 tbsp small haricot
    (navy) beans, soaked overnight
45–60ml/3–4 tbsp green
    split peas
45–60ml/3–4 tbsp yellow
    split peas
90–105ml/6–7 tbsp pearl barley
1 onion, chopped
2 carrots, sliced
3 celery sticks, diced or sliced
¹⁄₂ baking potato, peeled and cut
    into chunks
10g/¹⁄₄oz or 45ml/3 tbsp mixed
    dried mushrooms
5 garlic cloves, sliced
2 litres/3¹⁄₂ pints/8 cups water
2 vegetable stock (bouillon) cubes
salt and ground black pepper
30–45ml/2–3 tbsp chopped fresh
    parsley, to garnish

1 Put the beans, pearl barley, green and yellow split peas, onion, carrots, celery, potato, mushrooms, garlic and water into a large pan.

2 Bring the mixture to the boil, then reduce the heat, cover and simmer gently for about 1¹⁄₂ hours, or until the beans are completely tender.

3 Crumble the stock cubes into the soup, stir well and taste for seasoning. Ladle into warmed bowls, garnish with parsley and serve with rye or pumpernickel bread.

Cook's Tip
Do not add the stock cubes until the end of cooking, as the salt they contain will prevent the beans from becoming tender.

Hot Red Lentil Soup Energy 235kcal/991kJ; Protein 13g; Carbohydrate 28.4g, of which sugars 3.7g; Fat 8.9g, of which saturates 2.2g; Cholesterol 0mg; Calcium 66mg; Fibre 2.9g; Sodium 40mg.
Chunky Split Pea Energy 162kcal/689kJ; Protein 6.8g; Carbohydrate 34.1g, of which sugars 4.3g; Fat 0.8g, of which saturates 0.1g; Cholesterol 0mg; Calcium 34mg; Fibre 2.9g; Sodium 30mg.

Chunky Courgette and Potato Soup with Pasta

This is a delicious chunky vegetable soup from Nice in the south of France, served with tomato pesto and fresh Parmesan cheese. Serve in small portions as an appetizer, or in larger bowls with crusty bread as a filling lunch.

Serves 4–6

1 courgette (zucchini), diced
1 small potato, diced
1 shallot, chopped
1 carrot, diced
400g/14oz can chopped tomatoes
1.2 litres/2 pints/5 cups
    vegetable stock
50g/2oz French (green) beans, cut
    into 1cm/½in lengths
50g/2oz/½ cup frozen petits pois
    (baby peas)
50g/2oz/½ cup small
    pasta shapes
60–90ml/4–6 tbsp pesto
15ml/1 tbsp tomato
    purée (paste)
salt and ground black pepper
freshly grated Parmesan or
    Pecorino cheese, to serve

1 Place the courgette, potato, shallot, carrot and tomatoes, with the can juices, in a large pan. Add the stock and season well. Bring to the boil over a medium to high heat, then lower the heat, cover the pan and simmer for 20 minutes.

2 Bring the soup back to the boil and add the green beans and petits pois. Cook the mixture briefly, for about a minute. Add the pasta. Cook for a further 10 minutes, until the pasta is tender. Taste and adjust the seasoning.

3 Ladle the soup into bowls. Mix together the pesto and tomato purée, and stir a spoonful into each serving. Sprinkle with freshly grated Parmesan or Pecorino cheese.

> **Variation**
> To strengthen the tomato flavour, try using tomato-flavoured spaghetti, broken into small lengths, instead of the small pasta shapes. Sun-dried tomato purée (paste) can also be used instead of regular tomato purée.

Tuscan Bean and Potato Soup

There are lots of versions of this wonderful and very substantial soup, which makes a meal in itself. This one uses cannellini beans, potatoes, cabbage and good olive oil. It's a good idea to make it in advance of the meal, as it tastes even better when reheated.

Serves 4

45ml/3 tbsp extra virgin olive oil
1 onion, roughly chopped
2 leeks, roughly chopped
1 large potato, peeled and diced
2 garlic cloves, finely chopped
1.2 litres/2 pints/5 cups
    vegetable stock
400g/14oz can cannellini beans,
    drained, liquid reserved
175g/6oz Savoy cabbage,
    finely shredded
45ml/3 tbsp chopped fresh flat
    leaf parsley
30ml/2 tbsp chopped
    fresh oregano
75g/3oz/1 cup Parmesan
    cheese, shaved
salt and ground black pepper

For the garlic toasts
30–45ml/2–3 tbsp extra virgin
    olive oil
6 thick slices country bread
1 garlic clove, peeled
    and bruised

1 Heat the oil in a large pan and gently cook the onion, leeks, potato and garlic for 4–5 minutes.

2 Pour on the stock and liquid from the beans. Cover and simmer for 15 minutes.

3 Stir in the cabbage and beans with half the herbs, season and cook for 10 minutes more. Spoon about one-third of the soup into a food processor or blender and process until fairly smooth. Return to the soup in the pan, taste for seasoning and heat through for 5 minutes.

4 Meanwhile make the garlic toasts. Drizzle a little oil over the slices of bread, then rub both sides of each slice with the garlic. Toast until browned on both sides.

5 Ladle the soup into bowls. Sprinkle with the remaining herbs and the Parmesan shavings. Add a drizzle of olive oil and serve with the toasts.

Chunky Vegetable Energy 204kcal/857kJ; Protein 10.6g; Carbohydrate 23.6g, of which sugars 8.8g; Fat 8.1g, of which saturates 1.9g; Cholesterol 4mg; Calcium 150mg; Fibre 9.3g; Sodium 451mg.
Tuscan Bean Soup Energy 445kcal/1863kJ; Protein 18.9g; Carbohydrate 45.8g, of which sugars 9.3g; Fat 21.8g, of which saturates 6g; Cholesterol 19mg; Calcium 391mg; Fibre 9.1g; Sodium 707mg.

Peanut and Potato Soup

In this rich Latin-American soup, the peanuts and potatoes are used as a thickening agent, with unexpectedly delicious results.

Serves 6
60ml/4 tbsp groundnut (peanut) oil
1 onion, finely chopped
2 garlic cloves, crushed
1 red (bell) pepper, seeded and chopped
250g/9oz potatoes, peeled and diced
2 fresh red chillies, seeded and chopped
200g/7oz canned chopped tomatoes
150g/5oz/1¼ cups unsalted peanuts
1.5 litres/2½ pints/6¼ cups vegetable stock
salt and ground black pepper
30ml/2 tbsp chopped fresh coriander (cilantro), to garnish

1 Heat the oil in a large heavy pan over a low heat. Stir in the onion and cook for around 5 minutes, until soft. Add the garlic, pepper, potatoes, chillies and tomatoes. Stir well, cover and cook for 5 minutes.

2 Meanwhile, toast the peanuts by gently cooking them in a large dry frying pan. Turn and stir the peanuts until they are evenly golden. Take care not to burn them.

3 Set 30ml/2 tbsp of the peanuts aside for garnish. Grind the remaining nuts to a fine powder in a blender or food processor. Add the vegetables to the food processor and process until smooth. Return the mixture to the pan and stir in the vegetable stock. Bring to the boil, then lower the heat and simmer for 10 minutes.

4 Pour the soup into heated bowls. Garnish with a generous sprinkling of coriander and the remaining peanuts.

Cook's Tip
Replace the unsalted peanuts with peanut butter, if you like. Use equal quantities of chunky and smooth peanut butter for the ideal texture.

Spanish Potato and Garlic Soup

This classic Spanish potato and tomato soup is given a deliciously rich, tangy flavour by the addition of garlic and paprika.

Serves 6
30ml/2 tbsp olive oil
1 large onion, finely sliced
1 large potato, halved and cut into thin slices
4 garlic cloves, crushed
5ml/1 tsp paprika
400g/14oz can chopped tomatoes, drained
5ml/1 tsp thyme leaves
900ml/1½ pints/3¾ cups vegetable stock
5ml/1 tsp cornflour (cornstarch)
salt and ground black pepper
chopped thyme leaves, to garnish

1 Heat the oil in a large heavy pan and gently fry the onions, potato, garlic, and paprika for 5 minutes, until the onions have softened, but not browned.

2 Add the chopped tomatoes, thyme leaves and vegetable stock to the pan and bring the mixture slowly to the boil.

3 Reduce the heat and simmer the soup for 15–20 minutes until the potatoes have cooked through.

4 Mix the cornflour with a little water in a bowl to form a paste. Stir into the soup, then simmer for a further 5 minutes until the soup has thickened.

5 Using a wooden spoon, break the potatoes up slightly. Season to taste with salt and ground black pepper, then serve garnished with the chopped thyme leaves.

Cook's Tip
Making your own vegetable stock for this soup will result in a much better flavour. Simply add a selection of vegetables, such as onions, celery, leeks and carrots, and a few bay leaves to a large pan. Cover with water and bring to the boil, then simmer for about 30–45 minutes until the vegetables are soft and the water has taken on their flavours. Strain the stock.

Peanut and Potato Energy 260kcal/1079kJ; Protein 8g; Carbohydrate 14.7g, of which sugars 6.2g; Fat 19.2g, of which saturates 3.6g; Cholesterol 0mg; Calcium 30mg; Fibre 3g; Sodium 20mg.
Spanish Potato Energy 86kcal/359kJ; Protein 1.5g; Carbohydrate 11.5g, of which sugars 4.4g; Fat 4.1g, of which saturates 0.6g; Cholesterol 0mg; Calcium 15mg; Fibre 1.5g; Sodium 12mg.

Potato and Garlic Broth

Although there is plenty of garlic in this fragrant potato soup, it is not overpowering. Serve it piping hot with plenty of wholemeal bread, as the perfect winter warmer, or with one of the suggested accompaniments below.

Serves 4
2 small or 1 large head of garlic
   (about 20 cloves)
4 potatoes, diced
1.75 litres/3 pints/7½ cups
   vegetable stock
salt and ground black pepper
flat leaf parsley, to garnish

1 Preheat the oven to 190°C/375°F/Gas 5. Place the unpeeled garlic bulbs or bulb in a small roasting pan and bake for about 30 minutes until they are soft in the centre.

2 Meanwhile, place the potatoes in a large pan and pour in water to cover. Add a little salt, if needed. Bring to the boil, then reduce the heat, part-cover the pan and simmer for 10 minutes.

3 Meanwhile, simmer the stock for 5 minutes. Drain the potatoes and add them to the stock.

4 Squeeze the garlic pulp from the skins into the soup, reserving a few cloves to garnish. Stir and add seasoning to taste. Simmer the soup for a further 15 minutes before serving, garnished with whole garlic cloves and parsley.

Variations
• *Make the soup more substantial by toasting slices of French bread on one side, then topping the second sides with cheese and toasting until golden. Place a slice or two of toasted cheese in each bowl before ladling in the soup.*
• *Hot herb bread, with lots of chopped fresh parsley and plenty of grated lemon rind, is delicious with the broth. Mix the parsley and lemon rind with butter, and spread it between slices of French bread. Reshape the slices into a loaf and wrap in foil, then heat in the oven.*
• *You could roast shallots with the garlic, or sauté some celery to add to the simmering soup about 10 minutes before serving.*

Potato, Corn and Chilli Chowder

Corn, potatoes and chillies are traditional buddies, and here the cooling combination of creamed corn and milk is the perfect foil for the raging heat of the chillies.

Serves 6
2 tomatoes, skinned
1 onion, roughly chopped
375g/13oz can creamed corn
2 red (bell) peppers, halved
   and seeded
15ml/1 tbsp olive oil, plus extra
   for brushing
3 fresh red chillies, seeded
   and chopped
2 garlic cloves, chopped
5ml/1 tsp ground cumin
5ml/1 tsp ground coriander
600ml/1 pint/2½ cups milk
350ml/12fl oz/1½ cups
   vegetable stock
3 cobs of corn, kernels removed
450g/1lb potatoes, finely diced
60ml/4 tbsp double
   (heavy) cream
60ml/4 tbsp chopped
   fresh parsley
salt and ground black pepper

1 Process the tomatoes and onion in a food processor or blender to a smooth purée. Add the creamed corn and process again, then set aside. Preheat the grill to high.

2 Put the peppers, skin side up, on a grill (broiler) rack and brush with oil. Grill (broil) for 8–10 minutes, until the skins blacken and blister. Transfer to a bowl and cover with clear film (plastic wrap), then leave to cool. Peel and dice the peppers, then set aside.

3 Heat the oil in a large pan and add the chopped chillies and garlic. Cook, stirring, for 2–3 minutes, until softened.

4 Add the ground cumin and coriander, and cook for a further 1 minute. Stir in the corn purée and cook for about 8 minutes, stirring occasionally.

5 Pour in the milk and stock, then stir in the corn kernels, potatoes, red pepper and seasoning to taste. Cook for about 15–20 minutes, until the corn and potatoes are tender.

6 Pour the soup into deep bowls and add the cream, pouring it slowly into the middle of the bowls. Sprinkle with the chopped parsley and serve immediately.

Potato and Garlic Energy 115kcal/488kJ; Protein 4.3g; Carbohydrate 24.3g, of which sugars 2.1g; Fat 0.7g, of which saturates 0.2g; Cholesterol 0mg; Calcium 14mg; Fibre 2.3g; Sodium 219mg.
Corn and Chilli Energy 294kcal/1241kJ; Protein 8.9g; Carbohydrate 47.8g, of which sugars 20.8g; Fat 8.9g, of which saturates 4.8g; Cholesterol 20mg; Calcium 168mg; Fibre 4.2g; Sodium 299mg.

Goan Potato Soup with Samosas

Soup and vegetable samosas are ideal partners. Bought samosas are given an easy, but clever, flavour lift in this simple recipe.

Serves 4
60ml/4 tbsp sunflower oil
10ml/2 tsp black mustard seeds
1 large onion, chopped
1 fresh red chilli, seeded
  and chopped
2.5ml/½ tsp ground turmeric
1.5ml/¼ tsp cayenne pepper
900g/2lb potatoes, cut into cubes

4 fresh curry leaves
750ml/1¼ pint/3 cups
  vegetable stock
225g/8oz spinach leaves,
  torn if large
400ml/14fl oz/1⅔ cups
  coconut milk
handful of fresh coriander
  leaves (cilantro)
salt and black pepper

For the garlic samosas
1 large garlic clove, crushed
25g/1oz/2 tbsp butter
6 vegetable samosas

1 Heat the oil in a large pan. Add the mustard seeds, cover and cook until they begin to pop. Stir in the onion and chilli and cook for 5–6 minutes, until softened.

2 Stir in the turmeric, cayenne pepper, potatoes, curry leaves and stock. Bring to the boil, reduce the heat and cover the pan. Simmer for 15 minutes, stirring occasionally, until the potatoes are tender.

3 Meanwhile, prepare the samosas. Preheat the oven to 180°C/350°F/Gas 4. Melt the butter in a small pan with the garlic, stirring and crushing the garlic into the butter.

4 Place the samosas in an ovenproof dish – a gratin dish or quiche dish is ideal. Brush them lightly with the butter, turn them over and brush with the remaining butter. Heat through in the oven for about 5 minutes, until piping hot.

5 Add the spinach to the soup and cook for 5 minutes. Stir in the coconut milk and cook for a further 5 minutes.

6 Season and add the coriander leaves before ladling the soup into bowls. Serve with the garlic samosas.

Cinnamon-spiced Chickpea and Vegetable Soup

Cinnamon, ginger and turmeric are a warming mix of spices to perfectly complement earthy potatoes and nutty chickpeas.

Serves 6
1 large onion, chopped
1.2 litres/2 pints/5 cups
  vegetable stock
5ml/1 tsp ground cinnamon
5ml/1 tsp turmeric
15ml/1 tbsp grated fresh
  root ginger

pinch of cayenne pepper
2 carrots, diced
2 celery sticks, diced
400g/14oz can
  chopped tomatoes
450g/1lb floury potatoes, diced
pinch of saffron strands
400g/14oz can
  chickpeas, drained
30ml/2 tbsp chopped fresh
  coriander (cilantro)
15ml/1 tbsp lemon juice
salt and ground black pepper
fried wedges of lemon, to serve

1 Place the onion in a large pot with 300ml/½ pint/1¼ cups of the vegetable stock. Bring to the boil, reduce the heat and simmer gently for about 10 minutes.

2 Meanwhile, mix the cinnamon, turmeric, ginger, cayenne pepper and 30ml/2 tbsp of stock to form a paste. Stir into the onion mixture with the carrots, celery and remaining stock.

3 Bring to the boil, stirring constantly, and reduce the heat. Cover and simmer gently for 5 minutes.

4 Add the tomatoes and potatoes and heat until simmering gently again, then cover and cook for 20 minutes.

5 Add the saffron, chickpeas, coriander and lemon juice. Season to taste and heat briefly, then serve with fried wedges of lemon.

> **Cook's Tip**
> Shallow frying lemon wedges – or halves, if the fruit are small – caramelizes them, giving the juice a particularly rich flavour.

Goan Soup Energy 836kcal/3503kJ; Protein 16.7g; Carbohydrate 112g, of which sugars 8.6g; Fat 38.7g, of which saturates 4.9g; Cholesterol 0mg; Calcium 227mg; Fibre 8.9g; Sodium 117mg.
Chickpea Soup Energy 399kcal/1685kJ; Protein 20.6g; Carbohydrate 58.1g, of which sugars 4.1g; Fat 11g, of which saturates 1.4g; Cholesterol 0mg; Calcium 209mg; Fibre 10.8g; Sodium 101mg.

Tangy Sweet Potato and Red Pepper Soup

This delicious soup has a sweet and tangy flavour, as well as a wonderful colour thanks to the sweet potato and red pepper. The bonus is that it also tastes as good as it looks.

Serves 6

500g/1 1/4lb sweet potato
1 onion, roughly chopped
2 red (bell) peppers, about
 225g/8oz, seeded and cubed
2 large garlic cloves,
 roughly chopped
300ml/1/2 pint/1 1/4 cups dry
 white wine
1.2 litres/2 pints/5 cups vegetable
 stock
Tabasco sauce (optional)
sea salt and ground black pepper
country bread, to serve

1 Peel the sweet potato and cut it into cubes. Place the pieces in a large heavy pan with the red pepper, onion, garlic, white wine and vegetable or chicken stock.

2 Bring the mixture to the boil, then lower the heat and simmer the soup for about 25–30 minutes or until all the vegetables are quite soft.

3 Remove the pan from the heat and leave the soup to cool. Transfer the mixture to a blender and process until smooth.

4 Return the blended soup to the pan and reheat gently, if serving hot. Season to taste with salt, ground black pepper and a generous dash of Tabasco, if you like.

5 Pour the soup into a tureen or serving bowl and cool slightly. Serve warm or at room temperature, with plenty of thick, country-style bread.

> **Cook's Tip**
> For an attractive finish to this soup, try garnishing it with a sprinkling of finely diced bell pepper, if you like. Any colour will work well, whether red, green or yellow.

Sweet Potato and Parsnip Soup

The delicious combination of honeyed sweet potatoes and parsnips, two of the most popular root vegetables, is used in both the soup itself and, when roasted, also serves as a tasty garnish.

Serves 6

15ml/1 tbsp sunflower oil
1 large leek, sliced
2 celery sticks, chopped
450g/1 1b sweet potatoes, diced
225g/8oz parsnips, diced
900ml/1 1/2 pints/3 3/4 cups
 vegetable stock
salt and ground black pepper

For the garnish
15ml/1 tbsp chopped
 fresh parsley
roasted strips of sweet potatoes
 and parsnips

1 Heat the sunflower oil in a large pan and add the chopped leek, celery, sweet potatoes and parsnips. Cook gently for about 5 minutes, stirring to prevent them from browning or sticking to the pan.

2 Stir in the vegetable stock and slowly bring to the boil, then cover and simmer gently for about 25 minutes, or until the vegetables are tender, stirring occasionally. Season with salt and pepper to taste. Remove the pan from the heat and allow the soup to cool slightly.

3 Purée the soup in a food processor or blender until smooth, then return the soup to the pan and reheat gently.

4 Ladle the soup into warmed soup bowls to serve, and sprinkle over the chopped parsley and roasted strips of sweet potatoes and parsnips.

> **Cook's Tip**
> Making and freezing soup is a practical way of preserving a glut of root vegetables that are unlikely to keep well. Not only can excess raw vegetables be used this way, but leftover boiled, mashed or roasted root vegetables, can all be added to soup puréed, cooled or frozen.

Sweet Potato and Parsnip Energy 113kcal/479kJ; Protein 2.1g; Carbohydrate 21.6g, of which sugars 7.2g; Fat 2.6g, of which saturates 0.4g; Cholesterol 0mg; Calcium 45mg; Fibre 4.3g; Sodium 40mg.
Sweet Potato and Pepper Energy 121kcal/513kJ; Protein 1.6g; Carbohydrate 21.2g, of which sugars 7.9g; Fat 0.4g, of which saturates 0.1g; Cholesterol 0mg; Calcium 30mg; Fibre 2.7g; Sodium 37mg.

Simple Potato Wedges

These potato wedges are so easy to make, and can be served on their own with a garlic mayonnaise dip, or as an accompaniment to a more substantial meal. To make extra-spicy potato wedges, use chilli powder instead of paprika.

of paprika.
Serves 4
675g/1½lb floury potatoes, such as Maris Piper
45ml/3 tbsp olive oil
10ml/2 tsp paprika
5ml/1 tsp ground cumin
salt and ground black pepper

1 Preheat the oven to 190°C/375°F/Gas 5. Using a sharp knife, cut the potatoes into chunky wedges and place them in a roasting pan.

2 In a small bowl, combine the olive oil with the paprika and cumin and season with plenty of salt and ground black pepper.

3 Pour the spiced oil mixture over the potatoes and toss well to coat all the wedges thoroughly.

4 Spread the potatoes in a single layer in the roasting pan and bake in the preheated oven for about 30–40 minutes, or until golden brown and tender. Turn them once or twice during cooking to ensure they are evenly browned all over. Serve immediately.

Variation
If you prefer less spice in your food, substitute the paprika and cumin for finely chopped rosemary.

Cook's Tip
To make a garlic mayonnaise dip for the wedges, place 45ml–3 tbsp of good-quality mayonnaise in a bowl and stir in a crushed or finely chopped garlic clove. Season with a little salt and ground black pepper.

Potato Skins with Cajun Dip

Divinely crisp and decadent, these potato skins are great on their own, or served with this piquant dip as a garnish or to the side. They are delicious as a snack, or as an accompaniment to a barbecued feast.

Serves 2
2 large baking potatoes
vegetable oil, for deep frying

For the dip
120ml/4fl oz/½ cup natural (plain) yogurt
1 garlic clove, crushed
5ml/1 tsp tomato purée (paste)
2.5ml/½ tsp green chilli purée or ½ small green chilli, chopped
1.5ml/¼ tsp celery salt
salt and ground black pepper

1 Preheat the oven to 180°C/350°F/Gas 4. Bake the potatoes for 45–50 minutes until tender. Remove from the oven and set aside to cool slightly.

2 When the potatoes have cooled down enough to handle, cut them in half and scoop out the flesh, leaving a thin layer on the skins. Keep the flesh for another meal.

3 To make the dip, mix together all the ingredients and chill in the refrigerator until the skins are ready.

4 Heat a 1cm/½in layer of oil in a large pan or deep-fat fryer. Cut each potato half in half again, then fry them until crisp and golden on both sides.

5 Drain on kitchen paper, sprinkle with salt and black pepper and serve with a bowl of dip or a dollop of dip in each skin.

Cook's Tip
• If you prefer, you can microwave the potatoes to save time. This will take about 10 minutes.
• The scooped-out flesh from the potatoes is delicious if mixed with leftover vegetables such as peas or cabbage, then formed into small cakes and fried in a little oil until golden.

Potato Wedges Energy 200kcal/838kJ; Protein 3.3g; Carbohydrate 28.1g, of which sugars 2.2g; Fat 9.1g, of which saturates 1.4g; Cholesterol 0mg; Calcium 15mg; Fibre 1.7g; Sodium 20mg.
Potato Skins Energy 211kcal/873kJ; Protein 2.7g; Carbohydrate 12.5g, of which sugars 3.3g; Fat 17g, of which saturates 2.2g; Cholesterol 0mg; Calcium 62mg; Fibre 0.7g; Sodium 35mg.

Sweet Potato Crisps

You can use these sweet pink potatoes to make sweet or savoury crisps, and they have a lovely colour and a unique, almost fruity flavour. They are ideal as snacks at a party, or enjoy as a comforting supper treat.

Serves 4
2 medium sweet potatoes
vegetable oil, for deep-frying
salt

1 Using a vegetable peeler or knife, peel the sweet potatoes under cold running water.

2 Cut each sweet potato into 3mm/⅛in thick slices with a sharp knife or vegetable slicer and place in a bowl of salted cold water.

3 Heat a 1cm/½in layer of oil in a large pan or deep-fat fryer. While the oil is heating, remove the slices from the water and pat dry on kitchen paper.

4 When the oil is hot enough, fry a few potato slices at a time until crisp. Remove the slices from the pan with a slotted spoon and drain thoroughly on kitchen paper. Sprinkle with salt and serve warm.

Variation
For a sweet version, sprinkle with cinnamon and caster (superfine) sugar, and toss well, before cooling. You can prepare yams in just the same way.

Cook's Tip
These sweet potato crisps (chips) are delicious served warm, but if you don't manage to finish them in one sitting then they are equally good as a cold snack. Serve with a home-made dip, either sweet or savoury.

Potato Skewers with Mustard Dip

These potatoes are cooked on the barbecue and have a great flavour and a deliciously crisp skin. Try these tasty kebabs served with a thick, garlic-rich dip.

Serves 4
For the dip
4 garlic cloves, crushed
2 egg yolks

30ml/2 tbsp lemon juice
300ml/½ pint/1¼ cups extra virgin olive oil
10ml/2 tsp wholegrain mustard
salt and ground black pepper

For the skewers
1kg/2¼lb small new potatoes
200g/7oz shallots, halved
30ml/2 tbsp olive oil
15ml/1 tbsp sea salt

1 Prepare the barbecue for cooking the skewers before you begin. To make the dip, place the garlic, egg yolks and lemon juice in a blender or a food processor fitted with the metal blade and process for a few seconds until the mixture is throughly combined and smooth.

2 Keep the blender motor running and add the oil very gradually, pouring it in a thin stream, until the mixture forms a thick, glossy cream. Add the mustard and stir the ingredients together, then season with salt and black pepper. Chill until ready to use.

3 Par-boil the potatoes in their skins in boiling water for about 5 minutes. Drain well and then thread them on to metal skewers alternating with the shallots.

4 Brush the skewers with oil and sprinkle with salt. Cook over a barbecue for 10–12 minutes, turning occasionally. Serve immediately, accompanied by the dip.

Cook's Tips
• *New potatoes have a firmness necessary to stay on the skewer. Don't be tempted to use other types of small potato.*
• *These are just as delicious prepared under the grill (broiler): preheat the grill and continue as per step one above.*

Sweet Potato Crisps Energy 285kcal/1185kJ; Protein 1.2g; Carbohydrate 21.3g, of which sugars 5.7g; Fat 22.3g, of which saturates 2.4g; Cholesterol 0mg; Calcium 24mg; Fibre 2.4g; Sodium 40mg.
Potato Skewers Energy 488kcal/2024kJ; Protein 4.3g; Carbohydrate 29.5g, of which sugars 4.1g; Fat 40g, of which saturates 6.1g; Cholesterol 65mg; Calcium 28mg; Fibre 2.2g; Sodium 49mg.

Artichokes with New Potatoes

Among the first spring vegetables, artichokes appear in the middle of March. Together with new potatoes and other spring vegetables they make a delicious, healthy and unusual appetizer or snack.

Serves 4 as a first course

4 globe artichokes
juice of 1½ lemons
150ml/¼ pint/⅔ cup extra virgin
   olive oil
1 large onion, thinly sliced
3 carrots, peeled and sliced
   into long batons
300ml/½ pint/1¼ cups
   hot water
400g/14oz small new potatoes,
   scrubbed or peeled
4 or 5 spring onions (scallions),
   finely chopped
60–75ml/4–5 tbsp chopped
   fresh dill
salt and ground black pepper

1 Remove and discard the outer leaves of the artichoke until you reach the tender ones. Cut off the top, at around halfway down. Scoop out the hairy choke. Trim the stalk, leaving 4cm/1½in, and peel away its outer surface. Drop the artichokes into a bowl of cold water acidulated with about one-third of the lemon juice, which is about half a lemon. Add enough hot water to just about cover the artichokes.

2 Heat the extra virgin olive oil in a large, deep frying pan and gently cook the onion slices over a low to medium heat, stirring frequently, until they become translucent but not brown.

3 Add the carrots to the pan and cook for about 2–3 minutes. Stir in the remaining lemon juice and the hot water and bring the mixture to the boil.

4 Drain the artichokes and add them to the pan, followed by the potatoes, spring onions and seasoning. The vegetables should be almost covered with the sauce, so add a little more hot water if needed.

5 Cover and cook gently for about 45 minutes. Sprinkle over the dill and cook for 2–3 minutes more. Serve immediately.

Jerusalem Artichoke and Potato Rösti

A traditional potato dish, rösti is originally from Switzerland where it is often combined with other ingredients such as onion and egg. Here it has the addition of Jerusalem artichokes to create an unusual and tasty version, which works great as a snack or as a side dish.

Serves 4–6

450g/1lb Jerusalem artichokes
juice of 1 lemon
450g/1lb potatoes
about 50g/2oz/4 tbsp butter
salt

1 Peel the Jerusalem artichokes and place in a pan of water together with the lemon juice and a pinch of salt. Bring to the boil and cook for about 5 minutes until barely tender.

2 Peel the potatoes and place in a separate pan of salted water. Bring to the boil and cook until barely tender – the potatoes will take slightly longer than the artichokes.

3 Drain and cool the artichokes and potatoes, and then grate them into a bowl. Mix well, without breaking them up too much.

4 Melt the butter in a large heavy frying pan. Add the artichoke mixture, spreading it out with the back of a spoon. Cook gently for about 10 minutes.

5 Invert the 'cake' on to a plate and slide back into the pan. Cook for about 10 minutes until golden. Serve immediately.

> **Cook's Tip**
> Jerusalem artichokes are not a true artichoke but the root of a variety of sunflower. They may be labelled as sunroot or sunchoke.

> **Variation**
> Make individual rösti and serve topped with a mixed julienne of vegetables for an unusual first course.

Artichokes Energy 373kcal/1552kJ; Protein 5.6g; Carbohydrate 30.2g, of which sugars 13.7g; Fat 26.5g, of which saturates 3.9g; Cholesterol 0mg; Calcium 142mg; Fibre 6.7g; Sodium 103mg.
Artichoke Rösti Energy 119kcal/500kJ; Protein 1.7g; Carbohydrate 12.8g, of which sugars 1.7g; Fat 7.2g, of which saturates 4.6g; Cholesterol 19mg; Calcium 37mg; Fibre 1.6g; Sodium 116mg.

Wild Rice and Potato Rösti

This version of the Swiss potato dish features wild rice and a bright simple sauce.

Serves 6
90g/3½oz/½ cup wild rice
900g/2lb large potatoes
45ml/3 tbsp walnut oil
5ml/1 tsp yellow mustard seeds
1 onion, coarsely grated
  and drained

30ml/2 tbsp fresh thyme leaves
salt and ground black pepper
vegetables, to serve

For the purée
350g/12oz carrots, peeled and
  roughly chopped
pared rind and juice of
  1 large orange

1 For the purée, place the chopped carrots in a pan, cover with cold water and add two pieces of orange rind. Bring to the boil and cook for around 10 minutes, until the carrots are tender. Drain and discard the rind.

2 Purée the mixture in a food processor or blender with 60ml/4 tbsp of the orange juice. Return to the pan.

3 Place the wild rice in a clean pan and cover with water. Bring to the boil and cook for about 30–40 minutes, until the rice is just starting to split, but is still crunchy. Drain the rice.

4 Place the potatoes in a large pan and cover with cold water. Bring to the boil and cook for 10–15 minutes until just tender. Drain well and leave to cool slightly. Peel and coarsely grate them into a large bowl. Add the cooked rice.

5 Heat 30ml/2 tbsp of the oil in a frying pan and add the mustard seeds. When they start to pop, add the onion and cook gently for 5–7 minutes until soft. Add to the potato mixture, with the thyme, and mix thoroughly. Season to taste.

6 Heat the remaining oil and add the grated potato and rice mixture. Press down firmly to form a pancake and cook for 10 minutes or until golden brown. Cover the pan with a plate and flip over, then slide the rösti back in for another 10 minutes. Serve with the reheated carrot purée.

Gruyère and Potato Soufflés

This potato recipe can be prepared in advance if you are entertaining and given its second baking just before you serve it up.

Serves 4
225g/8oz floury potatoes
2 eggs, separated

175g/6oz/1½ cups Gruyère
  cheese, grated
50g/2oz/½ cup self-raising
  (self-rising) flour
50g/2oz spinach leaves
butter, for greasing
salt and freshly ground black
  pepper
salad leaves, to serve

1 Preheat the oven to 200°C/400°F/Gas 6. Cook the potatoes in lightly salted boiling water for around 20 minutes until very tender. Drain the potatoes and mash thoroughly before adding the two egg yolks and mixing to combine.

2 Stir in half of the Gruyère cheese and all of the flour. Season to taste with salt and pepper.

3 Finely chop the spinach leaves and gently fold into the potato and egg yolk mixture.

4 Whip the egg whites until they form soft peaks. Fold a little of the egg white into the mixture to loosen it slightly. Using a large metal spoon, fold the remaining egg white into the mixture.

5 Butter four large ramekin dishes. Pour the mixture in, place on a baking sheet and bake for 20 minutes. Remove from the oven and leave to cool.

6 Turn the soufflés out on to a baking sheet and sprinkle with the remaining cheese. Bake again for 5 minutes and serve immediately with salad leaves.

Variation
For a different flavouring, try replacing the Gruyère with a crumbled blue cheese, such as Stilton or Shropshire Blue cheeses, which have a more intense taste than the Gruyère.

Wild Rice Rösti Energy 235kcal/989kJ; Protein 4.2g; Carbohydrate 42.3g, of which sugars 7.6g; Fat 6.2g, of which saturates 0.7g; Cholesterol 0mg; Calcium 30mg; Fibre 3.1g; Sodium 32mg.
Gruyère Soufflés Energy 304kcal/1270kJ; Protein 16.7g; Carbohydrate 19g, of which sugars 1.2g; Fat 17.5g, of which saturates 10.4g; Cholesterol 138mg; Calcium 380mg; Fibre 1.2g; Sodium 376mg.

Indian Potato Pancakes

Although called a pancake, these crispy spiced potato cakes are more like a bhaji. They make a great appetizer before an Indian main course of curry and rice, as well as being ideal for a party buffet.

Makes 10
300g/11oz potatoes
25ml/1½ tsp garam masala or curry powder
4 spring onions (scallions), finely chopped
1 large egg white, lightly beaten
30ml/2 tbsp vegetable oil
salt and ground black pepper
selection of chutney and relishes, to serve

1 Peel the potatoes, then coarsely grate the flesh. Using your hands, squeeze the excess liquid from the grated potatoes and pat dry with kitchen paper.

2 Place the dry, grated potatoes in a separate bowl and add the spices, spring onions, egg white and seasoning. Stir the mixture until all the ingredients are well combined.

3 Heat a large, non-stick frying pan over a medium heat and add the vegetable oil.

4 Drop tablespoonfuls of the potato into the pan and flatten out with the back of a spoon (you will need to cook the pancakes in batches).

5 Cook for a few minutes and then flip the pancakes and continue cooking for a further 3 minutes until golden brown.

6 Drain the pancakes on kitchen paper and serve with a selection of chutney and relishes.

Cook's Tip
Wait until the last moment before grating the potatoes. If you prepare them too early before use, the flesh will quickly turn brown due to contact with the air.

Potato and Peanut Butter Fingers

Children will love these crispy, tasty peanut and potato croquettes. Make up a batch and freeze some ready for a quick midweek meal.

Makes 12
1kg/2¼lb potatoes
1 large onion, chopped
2 large (bell) peppers, red or green, chopped
3 carrots, coarsely grated
45ml/3 tbsp sunflower oil
2 courgettes (zucchini), coarsely grated
115g/4oz mushrooms, chopped
15ml/1 tbsp dried mixed herbs
115g/4oz mature (sharp) Cheddar cheese, grated
75g/3oz/½ cup crunchy peanut butter
salt and ground black pepper
2 eggs, beaten
about 50g/2oz/1 cup dried breadcrumbs
45ml/3 tbsp Parmesan cheese
oil, for deep frying

1 Cook the potatoes in plenty of boiling water until tender, then drain well and mash. Set aside.

2 Fry the onion, peppers and carrots gently in the sunflower oil for about 5 minutes, then add the courgettes and mushrooms. Cook for a further 5 minutes.

3 Mix the potato with the dried mixed herbs, grated cheese and peanut butter. Season with salt and ground black pepper to taste. Leave the mixture to cool for 30 minutes, then stir in one of the eggs.

4 Spread out on a large plate, cool and chill, then divide into 12 portions and shape. Dip your hands in cold water if the mixture sticks.

5 Put the second egg in a bowl and dip the potato fingers into it first, then into the crumbs and Parmesan cheese until coated evenly. Return the fingers to the refrigerator until set.

6 Heat oil in a deep fat fryer to 190°C/375°F/Gas 5, then fry the fingers in batches for about 3 minutes until golden. Drain well on kitchen paper. Serve immediately.

Indian Pancakes Energy 50kcal/210kJ; Protein 1.3g; Carbohydrate 5.8g, of which sugars 0.5g; Fat 2.6g, of which saturates 0.3g; Cholesterol 0mg; Calcium 8mg; Fibre 0.4g; Sodium 11mg.
Peanut Fingers Energy 269kcal/1120kJ; Protein 8.3g; Carbohydrate 23.3g, of which sugars 6.6g; Fat 16.3g, of which saturates 4.2g; Cholesterol 41mg; Calcium 110mg; Fibre 2.9g; Sodium 151mg.

Potato Cakes with Stuffing

Only a few communities in India make these unusual potato cakes. Serve them as a tasty appetizer, or they can also be served as a main meal, accompanied by a fresh tomato salad.

Makes 8–10
15ml/1 tbsp vegetable oil
1 large onion, finely chopped
2 garlic cloves, finely crushed
5cm/2in piece fresh root ginger, finely crushed
5ml/1 tsp ground coriander
5ml/1 tsp ground cumin
2 fresh green chillies, finely chopped

30ml/2 tbsp each chopped fresh coriander (cilantro) and mint
225g/8oz minced (ground) Quorn
50g/2oz/⅓ cup frozen peas, thawed
juice of 1 lemon
900g/2lb potatoes, boiled and mashed
2 eggs, beaten
dry breadcrumbs, for coating
vegetable oil, for shallow-frying
salt
lemon wedges and salad leaves, to serve

1 Heat the oil and fry the onion, garlic, ginger, coriander, cumin, chillies and fresh coriander until the onion is translucent.

2 Add the Quorn and peas and fry well until the meat is cooked, then season to taste with salt and lemon juice. The mixture should be very dry.

3 Divide the mashed potato into 8–10 portions, take one portion at a time and flatten into a pancake in the palm of your hand. Place a spoonful of the meat in the centre and gather the sides together to enclose the meat. Flatten it slightly to make a round.

4 Dip the cakes in beaten egg and then coat in breadcrumbs. Set aside to chill in the refrigerator for about 1 hour until they have firmed up slightly.

5 Heat the oil in a frying pan and shallow-fry the cakes until brown and crisp all over. Serve them hot with lemon wedges on a bed of salad leaves.

Potato Cakes with Feta Cheese

Yummy little fried mouthfuls of potato and tangy-sharp Greek feta cheese, flavoured with dill and lemon juice. Serve as an appetizer or party bite.

Serves 4
500g/1¼lb floury potatoes
115g/4oz/1 cup feta cheese
4 spring onions (scallions), finely chopped

45ml/3 tbsp chopped fresh dill
1 egg, beaten
15ml/1 tbsp lemon juice
salt and ground black pepper
plain (all-purpose) flour, for dredging
45ml/3 tbsp olive oil
dill sprigs, to garnish
shredded spring onions (scallions), to garnish
lemon wedges, to serve

1 Cook the potatoes in their skins in boiling, lightly salted water until soft. Drain and leave to cool slightly, then chop them in half and peel while still warm.

2 Place the potatoes in a bowl and mash. Crumble the feta cheese into the potatoes, add the spring onions, dill, egg and lemon juice and season with salt and pepper. (The cheese is salty, so taste before you add salt.) Stir well.

3 Cover the bowl and chill in the refrigerator until the mixture is firm. Divide the mixture into walnut-size balls, then flatten them slightly. Dredge with flour, shaking off the excess.

4 Heat the oil in a heavy frying pan and fry the cakes in batches until golden brown, about 3–5 minutes on both sides. Keep the cooked cakes warm while you use up the mixture. Drain well on kitchen paper and serve hot, garnished with spring onions, dill and lemon wedges.

> **Cook's Tip**
> *Ensure that you use floury varieties of potato for this dish rather than waxy potatoes, such as new or salad potatoes. Look out for varieties such as Golden Wonder, Maris Piper, Estima and King Edward.*

Stuffed Potato Cakes Energy 260kcal/1086kJ; Protein 10.6g; Carbohydrate 21.3g, of which sugars 3.4g; Fat 15.4g, of which saturates 3.6g; Cholesterol 88mg; Calcium 29mg; Fibre 1.9g; Sodium 62mg.
Feta Potato Cakes Energy 263kcal/1098kJ; Protein 8.6g; Carbohydrate 22.8g, of which sugars 2.4g; Fat 15.9g, of which saturates 5.6g; Cholesterol 68mg; Calcium 126mg; Fibre 1.5g; Sodium 446mg.

The Simplest Potato Salad

The secret of this potato salad is to mix the potatoes with the dressing while they are still hot so that they absorb its flavours. This is perfect with a colourful selection of roasted vegetables.

Serves 4–6
675g/1½lb small new or
    salad potatoes
4 spring onions (scallions)
45ml/3 tbsp olive oil
15ml/1 tbsp white wine vinegar
175ml/6fl oz/¾ cup good
    mayonnaise, preferably
    home-made
45ml/3 tbsp chopped chives
salt and ground black pepper

1 Cook the potatoes in their skins in a large pan of boiling salted water until tender.

2 Meanwhile, wash the spring onions, then finely chop the white parts along with a little of the green parts; they look more attractive cut on the diagonal. Set aside the chopped onions until ready to use.

3 Whisk together the olive oil and wine vinegar. Drain the potatoes well and place them in a large bowl, then immediately toss lightly with the prepared dressing and the spring onions. Put the bowl to one side to cool.

4 Gently stir the mayonnaise and chopped chives into the potatoes, season well with salt and ground black pepper and chill thoroughly until ready to serve. Adjust the seasoning before serving, if necessary.

Cook's Tips
• *When making dressings, instead of whisking the ingredients in a bowl, simply place them in a screw-top jar and give it a good shake to combine.*
• *This is the perfect dish for a picnic or barbecue, as it can be made well ahead and is served chilled. If you want to do this, add the mayonnaise and chives just before serving.*

Potatoes with Egg and Lemon Dressing

This potato favourite takes on a new lease of life when mixed with hard-boiled eggs and lemon juice. With its tangy flavour, this is the ideal salad to accompany a summer barbecue.

Serves 4
900g/2lb new potatoes
1 small onion, finely chopped
2 hard-boiled eggs, shelled
300ml/½ pint/1¼ cups
    mayonnaise
1 garlic clove, crushed
finely grated rind and juice
    of 1 lemon
60ml/4 tbsp chopped fresh
    parsley, plus extra
    for garnishing
salt and ground black pepper

1 Scrub or scrape the potatoes. Put them in a pan, cover with cold water and add a pinch of salt. Bring to the boil, then simmer for 15 minutes, or until tender.

2 Drain and leave to cool. Cut the potatoes into large dice, season with salt and pepper and combine with the onion.

3 Halve the eggs and set aside the yolk. Roughly chop the whites and place in a mixing bowl. Stir in the mayonnaise. Mix the garlic, lemon rind and lemon juice in a small bowl and stir into the mayonnaise mixture, combining thoroughly.

4 Stir the mayonnaise mixture into the potatoes, coating them well, then fold in the chopped parsley. Press the egg yolk through a sieve (strainer) and sprinkle on top. Serve cold or chilled, garnished with parsley.

Variation
For a change, replace the potato with cooked beetroot (beets). The mayonnaise will turn bright pink, which may surprise your guests, but the flavour is excellent. Alternatively, use a mixture of potatoes and beetroot.

Simplest Potato Salad Energy 206kcal/863kJ; Protein 2.8g; Carbohydrate 24.3g, of which sugars 2.1g; Fat 11.5g, of which saturates 1.7g; Cholesterol 0mg; Calcium 22mg; Fibre 1.8g; Sodium 19mg.
Potatoes with Egg Energy 723kcal/3000kJ; Protein 8.4g; Carbohydrate 39.1g, of which sugars 5.1g; Fat 60.4g, of which saturates 9.6g; Cholesterol 151mg; Calcium 68mg; Fibre 3.2g; Sodium 403mg.

Deli Potato Salad with Egg, Mayonnaise and Olives

Potato salad is synonymous with deli food and there are many varieties, some with sour cream, some with vinaigrette and others with vegetables. This tasty version includes a piquant mustard mayonnaise, chopped eggs and green olives.

Serves 6–8

1kg/2¼lb waxy salad
  potatoes, scrubbed
1 red, brown or white onion,
  finely chopped
2–3 celery sticks, finely chopped
60–90ml/4–6 tbsp chopped
  fresh parsley
15–20 pimiento-stuffed
  olives, halved
3 hard-boiled eggs, chopped
60ml/4 tbsp extra virgin
  olive oil
60ml/4 tbsp white
  wine vinegar
15–30ml/1–2 tbsp mild or
  wholegrain mustard
celery seeds, to taste (optional)
175–250ml/6–8fl oz/¾–1 cup
  mayonnaise
salt and ground black pepper
paprika, to garnish

1 Put the potatoes in a pan, pour in water to cover and add a pinch of salt. Bring to the boil, then reduce the heat and cook gently for about 10 minutes, or until the potatoes are just tender. Drain well and return to the pan. Leave for 2–3 minutes to cool and dry a little.

2 When the potatoes are cool enough to handle but still very warm, cut them with a sharp knife into chunks or slices and place in a salad bowl.

3 Sprinkle the potatoes with salt and ground black pepper, then add the onion, celery, parsley, olives and the chopped eggs.

4 Place the olive oil in a small bowl, then whisk in the vinegar, mustard and celery seeds, if using. Pour the dressing over the salad and toss to combine.

5 Stir in enough mayonnaise to bind the salad together. Chill in the refrigerator before serving. Sprinkle with a little paprika when you are ready to serve.

Potato and Olive Salad

This delicious salad is simple and zesty – the perfect choice for lunch, as an accompaniment, or as an appetizer. Similar in appearance to flat leaf parsley, fresh coriander has a distinctive pungent, almost spicy flavour. It is widely used in India, the Middle and Far East and in eastern Mediterranean countries. This unusual potato salad is particularly good served as part of a decadent brunch.

Serves 4

8 large new potatoes
45–60ml/3–4 tbsp garlic-flavoured
  oil and vinegar dressing
60–90ml/4–6 tbsp chopped fresh
  herbs, such as coriander
  (cilantro) and chives
10–15 dry-fleshed black
  Mediterranean olives

1 Cut the new potatoes into chunks. Put them in a pan, pour in water to cover and add a pinch of salt. Bring to the boil, then reduce the heat and cook gently for about 10 minutes.

2 When the potatoes are just tender, drain well and leave in a colander to dry thoroughly and cool slightly.

3 When the potatoes are cool enough to handle, chop them into bitesize chunks and place them in a serving bowl.

4 Drizzle the garlic dressing over the potatoes. Toss well until the pieces are evenly coated and sprinkle with the chopped fresh coriander, chives, and black olives. Mix well until all the ingredients are well combined. Chill in the refrigerator for at least 1 hour before serving.

> **Variations**
> • If you like your food a little spicier, add a pinch of ground cumin or a sprinkling of roasted whole cumin seeds to the salad before serving.
> • Try different flavoured dressings, if you like, in place of the garlic version. Those flavoured with mustard, chilli or herbs, will work equally well.

Deli Potato Salad Energy 323kcal/1343kJ; Protein 5.2g; Carbohydrate 21.5g, of which sugars 2.7g; Fat 24.7g, of which saturates 4g; Cholesterol 88mg; Calcium 49mg; Fibre 2g; Sodium 149mg.
Potato and Olive Salad Energy 132kcal/548kJ; Protein 1.9g; Carbohydrate 12.4g, of which sugars 1.2g; Fat 8.6g, of which saturates 1.3g; Cholesterol 0mg; Calcium 42mg; Fibre 2g; Sodium 575mg.

Warm Hazelnut and Pistachio Salad

Two kinds of crunchy nuts turn ordinary potato salad into a really special accompaniment. This would be lovely as part of a vegetarian buffet, but you can also serve it on its own as a healthy snack.

Serves 4
900g/2lb small new or
   salad potatoes

30ml/2 tbsp hazelnut or
   walnut oil
60ml/4 tbsp sunflower oil
juice of 1 lemon
25g/1oz/¼ cup hazelnuts,
   shells removed
15 pistachio nuts, shells removed
salt and ground black pepper
flat leaf parsley sprig, to garnish

1 Cook the potatoes in their skins in boiling salted water for about 10–15 minutes until tender.

2 Drain the potatoes well in a colander and leave them to cool slightly.

3 Meanwhile, mix together the hazelnut or walnut oil with the sunflower oil and lemon juice. Season well with salt and ground black pepper.

4 Using a sharp knife, roughly chop the shelled hazelnuts and the pistachio nuts.

5 Put the cooled potatoes into a large bowl and pour the dressing over. Toss to combine.

6 Sprinkle the salad with the chopped nuts. Serve immediately, garnished with flat leaf parsley.

> **Variation**
> Use chopped walnuts in place of the hazelnuts, if you like. Try to buy the broken pieces of nut, which are less expensive than walnut halves, but chop them into smaller pieces before adding them to the salad.

Ensaladilla

A Spanish version of what is commonly known as Russian salad, this potato dish is a meal in itself.

Serves 4
8 new potatoes, scrubbed
   and quartered
1 large carrot, diced
115g/4oz fine green beans,
   cut into 2cm/¾in lengths
75g/3oz/¾ cup peas
½ Spanish onion, chopped
4 cornichons or small
   gherkins, sliced
1 small red (bell) pepper, seeded
   and diced

50g/2oz/½ cup pitted
   black olives
15ml/1 tbsp drained
   pickled capers
15ml/1 tbsp freshly squeezed
   lemon juice
30ml/2 tbsp chopped fresh fennel
   or parsley
salt and ground black pepper

For the aioli
2 garlic cloves, finely chopped
2.5ml/½ tsp salt
150ml/¼ pint/⅔ cup
   mayonnaise

1 To make the aioli, crush the garlic with the salt in a mortar with a pestle, then whisk or stir into the mayonnaise.

2 Cook the potatoes and diced carrot in a pan of boiling, lightly salted water for 5–8 minutes until almost tender. Add the beans and peas to the pan and cook for 2 minutes, or until all the vegetables are tender. Drain well.

3 Transfer the vegetables to a large bowl. Add the onion, cornichons or gherkins, red pepper, olives and capers. Stir in the aioli and season to taste with pepper and lemon juice.

4 Toss the vegetables and aioli together, adjust the seasoning and chill well. Serve garnished with fennel or parsley.

> **Variation**
> This salad is delicious using any combination of chopped, cooked vegetables. Work with the calendar and use fresh seasonal ingredients.

Warm Hazelnut Salad Energy 369kcal/1541kJ; Protein 5.4g; Carbohydrate 36.9g, of which sugars 3.4g; Fat 23.2g, of which saturates 2.6g; Cholesterol 0mg; Calcium 27mg; Fibre 2.9g; Sodium 45mg.
Ensaladilla Energy 397kcal/1645kJ; Protein 4.9g; Carbohydrate 25.3g, of which sugars 7.8g; Fat 31.4g, of which saturates 4.9g; Cholesterol 28mg; Calcium 47mg; Fibre 4.4g; Sodium 609mg.

New Potato and Quail's Egg Salad

Freshly cooked quail's eggs and tender waxy potatoes mix perfectly in this salad with the flavours of celery salt and the peppery-tasting rocket leaves. If you prefer your salad a little spicier, then replace the paprika with chilli powder.

Serves 6
900g/2lb new potatoes
50g/2oz/¼ cup butter
15ml/1 tbsp chopped chives
a pinch of celery salt
a pinch of paprika
12 quail's eggs
a few rocket (arugula) leaves
salt and ground black pepper
chopped chives, to garnish

1 Boil the potatoes in a large pan of salted water for about 20 minutes or until tender.

2 Meanwhile, beat the butter and chives together with the celery salt and the paprika.

3 While the potatoes are cooking, boil the eggs for 3 minutes, then drain and plunge into a bowl of cold water. Peel the eggs under running water.

4 Arrange the rocket leaves on individual plates or a serving platter and top with the eggs.

5 Drain the potatoes and add the seasoned butter. Toss well to melt the butter and carefully spoon the potatoes on to the plates of rocket and egg. Garnish the salad with a few of the remaining chopped chives and serve immediately.

Cook's Tips
• *You can buy bags of distinctive peppery rocket (arugula), on its own, or mixed with other leaves, in many supermarkets. It is also easy to grow from seed and makes a worthwhile and versatile addition to a herb patch.*
• *Tiny quail's eggs are available from larger supermarkets and butchers. They make an attractive addition to any salad. If unavailable, use hen's eggs, quartered.*

Beetroot and Potato Salad

A brightly coloured potato salad with a lovely texture. The sweetness of the beetroot contrasts perfectly with the tangy dressing. It is the ideal salad to serve with roasted vegetable cous cous.

Serves 4
4 medium beetroot (beets)
4 potatoes, peeled and diced

1 red onion, finely chopped
150ml/¼ pint/⅔ cup natural (plain) yogurt
10ml/2 tsp cider vinegar
2 small sweet and sour cucumbers, finely chopped
10ml/2 tsp creamed horseradish
salt and ground black pepper
parsley sprigs, to garnish

1 Trim the leafy stalks of the beetroot down to about 2.5cm/1 in of the root. Wash, but do not peel, the beetroot. Boil the unpeeled beetroot in a large pan of water for 40 minutes or until tender.

2 Meanwhile, boil the diced potatoes in a separate pan for 20 minutes until just tender.

3 When the beetroot are cooked, rinse and remove the skins. Chop into rough pieces and place in a bowl. Drain the potatoes and add to the bowl, together with the onions.

4 Mix the yogurt, vinegar, cucumbers and horseradish. Reserve a little for a garnish and pour the remainder over the salad. Toss and serve with parsley sprigs and the remaining dressing.

Cook's Tip
If you are short of time, buy vacuum-packed, ready-cooked and peeled beetroot, available in most supermarkets.

Variation
Add a few toasted chopped hazelnuts or walnuts to the yogurt dressing, if you like.

Potato and Egg Salad Energy 204kcal/855kJ; Protein 5.7g; Carbohydrate 24.2g, of which sugars 2g; Fat 10.1g, of which saturates 5.3g; Cholesterol 113mg; Calcium 25mg; Fibre 1.5g; Sodium 102mg.
Beetroot and Potato Energy 141kcal/597kJ; Protein 5.8g; Carbohydrate 28.8g, of which sugars 12.9g; Fat 1.2g, of which saturates 0.3g; Cholesterol 1mg; Calcium 107mg; Fibre 3.4g; Sodium 144mg.

Italian Potato Salad

A combination of antipasto ingredients and potatoes makes this a very substantial and delicious dish. It is a great side dish to grilled halloumi, or is hearty enough to serve on its own as a vegetarian treat.

Serves 6
1 aubergine (eggplant), sliced
75ml/5 tbsp olive oil

2 garlic cloves, cut into slivers
4 sun-dried tomatoes in oil, halved
2 red (bell) peppers, halved,
  seeded and cut into
  large chunks
2 large baking potatoes,
  cut into wedges
10ml/2 tsp mixed dried
  Italian herbs
30–45ml/2–3 tbsp
  balsamic vinegar
salt and ground black pepper

1 Preheat the oven to 200°C/400°F/Gas 6. Place the aubergine slices in a medium roasting pan with the olive oil, garlic and sun-dried tomatoes. Lay the pepper chunks over the top of the aubergine slices.

2 Arrange the potato wedges on top of the other ingredients in the roasting pan. Sprinkle the mixed herbs over the vegetables and season with salt and plenty of ground black pepper. Tightly cover the pan with foil and bake in the oven for about 45 minutes.

3 Remove the pan from the oven and turn the vegetables over. Then return to the oven and cook, with the foil removed, for about 30 minutes, until the vegetables are tender and browned.

4 Transfer the vegetables to a serving dish with a slotted spoon. Add the vinegar and seasoning to the pan, whisk and pour over the vegetables. Garnish with salt and black pepper.

Variation
This is a versatile recipe and it is worth experimenting with other vegetables to accompany the potato wedges. Try using slices of courgettes (zucchini), red onion wedges, green (bell) peppers or slices of fennel bulb.

Beetroot, Apple and Potato Salad

This salad is from Finland, where it is known as rosolli. It is served on Christmas Eve, just as the festive excitement mounts. The sweet apple and beetroot are the perfect partner for potatoes, pickled gherkins and eggs.

Serves 4
1 apple
3 cooked potatoes, finely diced

2 large gherkins, finely diced
3 cooked beetroots (beet),
  finely diced
3 cooked carrots, finely diced
1 onion, finely chopped
500ml/17fl oz/generous 2 cups
  double (heavy) cream
3 hard-boiled eggs,
  roughly chopped
15ml/1 tbsp chopped
  fresh parsley
salt and ground white pepper

1 Cut the apple into small dice. Place the pieces into a large bowl and add the diced potatoes, gherkins, beetroot, carrots and onion. Season the ingredients with plenty of salt and ground black pepper.

2 Carefully mix together all the ingredients in the bowl until they are well combined. Spoon the mixture into individual serving bowls.

3 Place the double cream into a separate bowl. Add any juice from the diced beetroot into the cream to give it additional flavour and an attractive pinkish colour. Stir well until the juice and cream are thoroughly combined.

4 Spoon the beetroot cream over the chopped vegetables and apple. Sprinkle the chopped eggs and parsley over the top of each portion before serving.

Variation
Stir a handful of feta cheese cubes into the mixture with the chopped parsley to add an extra dimension to the dish. Omit the added salt if you add the cheese, as it will be salty itself.

Italian Salad Energy 154kcal/644kJ; Protein 2.2g; Carbohydrate 15.6g, of which sugars 3.1g; Fat 9.7g, of which saturates 1.5g; Cholesterol 0mg; Calcium 12mg; Fibre 2.2g; Sodium 17mg.
Beetroot Potato Salad Energy 717kcal/2959kJ; Protein 8.5g; Carbohydrate 11g, of which sugars 10.2g; Fat 71.5g, of which saturates 42.9g; Cholesterol 314mg; Calcium 114mg; Fibre 2.3g; Sodium 132mg.

Potato and Feta Salad

This flavourful potato salad is quick and simple to assemble, making it ideal for a lunch or dinner dish on a busy day.

Serves 4
115g/4oz feta cheese
500g/1¼lb small new potatoes
5 spring onions (scallions), green and white parts finely chopped
15ml/1 tbsp rinsed bottled capers
8–10 black olives
45ml/3 tbsp finely chopped fresh flat leaf parsley
30ml/2 tbsp finely chopped mint
salt and ground black pepper

For the dressing
90–120ml/6–8 tbsp extra virgin olive oil
juice of 1 lemon, or to taste
45ml/3 tbsp Greek (US strained plain) yogurt
45ml/3 tbsp finely chopped fresh dill, plus a few sprigs, to garnish
5ml/1 tsp French mustard

1 Chop the feta cheese into small, even cubes and crumble slightly into a bowl. Set aside.

2 Bring a pan of lightly salted water to the boil and cook the potatoes in their skins for 25–30 minutes, or until tender. Take care not to let them become soggy and disintegrate. Drain them thoroughly and let them cool a little.

3 When the potatoes are cool enough to handle, peel them with your fingers and place them in a large bowl. If they are very small, keep them whole; otherwise cut them into large, even cubes. Add the chopped spring onions, capers, olives, feta cheese and fresh herbs, then toss gently wth salad tongs to mix thoroughly.

4 To make the dressing, place the extra virgin olive oil in a bowl with the lemon juice. Whisk thoroughly for a few minutes until the dressing emulsifies and thickens; you may need to add a little more olive oil if it does not thicken.

5 Whisk in the yogurt, dill and mustard, with salt and pepper to taste. Dress the salad while the potatoes are still warm, tossing lightly to coat them.

Feta and Mint Potato Salad

The oddly named pink fir apple potatoes are perfect for this salad, and taste great with feta cheese, yogurt and fresh mint. This dish goes very well with savoury vegetarian tarts and quiches.

Serves 4
500g/1¼ lb pink fir apple potatoes
90g/3½ oz feta cheese, crumbled

For the dressing
225g/8oz/1 cup natural (plain) yogurt
15g/½oz/½ cup fresh mint leaves
30ml/2 tbsp mayonnaise
salt and ground black pepper

1 Steam the potatoes over a pan of boiling water for about 20 minutes, until tender.

2 Meanwhile, make the dressing. Mix together the yogurt and mint, place in a food processor and pulse until the mint leaves are finely chopped. Scrape the blended mixture into a small bowl, stir in the mayonnaise and season to taste with salt and pepper.

3 Drain the potatoes well and transfer them to a large bowl. Spoon the dressing over the potatoes and scatter the feta cheese on top. Serve immediately.

Cook's Tip
Pink fir apple potatoes have a smooth waxy texture and retain their shape when cooked. Charlotte, Belle de Fontenay and other special salad potatoes could be used instead.

Variations
• *Crumbled Kefalotiri or young Manchego could be used instead of the feta.*
• *For a richer dressing, use Greek (US strained plain) yogurt.*

Potato and Feta Salad Energy 138kcal/566kJ; Protein 1.3g; Carbohydrate 1.2g, of which sugars 1.1g; Fat 14.2g, of which saturates 2g; Cholesterol 0mg; Calcium 75mg; Fibre 1.4g; Sodium 40mg.
Feta and Mint Potato Salad Energy 229kcal/959kJ; Protein 8.7g; Carbohydrate 25g, of which sugars 6.3g; Fat 11.2g, of which saturates 4.4g; Cholesterol 22mg; Calcium 204mg; Fibre 1.3g; Sodium 419mg.

Pasta, Asparagus and Potato Salad

This delicious wholewheat pasta and potato salad is a real treat, especially when made with fresh asparagus that is just in season.

60ml/4 tbsp extra virgin olive oil
350g/12oz baby new potatoes
225g/8oz asparagus
115g/4oz piece Parmesan cheese
salt and ground black pepper

Serves 4
225g/8oz wholewheat pasta
  shapes, such as fusilli

1 Cook the pasta in a pan of salted, boiling water for about 10–12 minutes, or according to the instructions on the packet, until it is al dente.

2 Drain well and toss with the olive oil while the pasta is still warm. Season with salt and ground black pepper.

3 Scrub the potatoes and cook in boiling salted water for about 15 minutes, or until tender. Drain the potatoes and toss together with the pasta.

4 Trim any woody ends off the asparagus and halve the stalks if very long. Blanch in boiling salted water for 6 minutes, until bright green and still crunchy. Drain well. Plunge into cold water to stop the asparagus cooking and allow to cool. Drain and dry on kitchen paper.

5 Toss the asparagus with the potatoes and pasta, adjust the seasoning to taste and transfer to a serving bowl. Using a vegetable peeler, shave the Parmesan over the salad and serve.

Cook's Tip
Asparagus only has a short season in most areas, usually for one or two months in spring and early summer – although greenhouse-grown asparagus may be available longer in some regions. It is grown in sandy soil, so wash thoroughly before use to ensure there is no grit in the spearheads.

Potato and Curry Plant Salad

This tasty and unusual potato salad is heightened by the distinctive and delicious aroma of curry plant leaves. This salad can be prepared well in advance and is therefore a useful dish to make for a buffet or picnic.

Serves 6
1kg/2lb new potatoes, in skins
300ml/½ pint/1¼ cups
  store-bought mayonnaise
6 curry plant leaves,
  roughly chopped
salt and ground black pepper
mixed lettuce or other salad
  greens, to serve

1 Place the potatoes in a pan of salted water and boil for about 15 minutes or until tender. Drain in a colander and place in a large bowl to cool slightly.

2 Meanwhile, make the dressing. In a separate bowl, mix together the mayonnaise with the curry plant leaves and ground black pepper.

3 Add the dressing to the potatoes while they are still warm. Stir until the ingredients are well combined and the potatoes are evenly coated. Season to taste with a little salt and some more ground black pepper, if necessary.

4 Leave the salad to cool to room temperature, then serve on a bed of mixed lettuce or other assorted salad leaves.

Cook's Tips
• *The curry plant is a shrub of the daisy family from southern Europe. It is so called because its silvery needle-like leaves have a mild curry flavour. The leaves can be used in a similar way to other woody herbs such as rosemary. It should not be confused with curry leaves.*
• *The quality of the mayonnaise is important to this recipe. Buy the best version you can find.*
• *Curry plant leaves can lose their potency when dried; to make the most of their distinctive aroma, always try and find fresh leaves. They have a short shelf-life but freeze well.*

Potato and Curry Leaf Salad Energy 342kcal/1421kJ; Protein 2.9g; Carbohydrate 21g, of which sugars 3.1g; Fat 28g, of which saturates 4.3g; Cholesterol 27mg; Calcium 27mg; Fibre 1.8g; Sodium 178mg.
Pasta and Potato Salad Energy 487kcal/2042kJ; Protein 22g; Carbohydrate 52.5g, of which sugars 4.3g; Fat 22.4g, of which saturates 7.8g; Cholesterol 29mg; Calcium 383mg; Fibre 6.6g; Sodium 397mg.

New Potato Spring Salad

This potato salad makes a satisfying meal. You could also use other spring vegetables, if you like.

Serves 4

675g/1½lb small new potatoes, halved
400g/14oz can broad (fava) beans, drained
115g/4oz cherry tomatoes
50g/2oz/⅓ cup walnut halves
30ml/2 tbsp white wine vinegar
15ml/1 tbsp wholegrain mustard
60ml/4 tbsp olive oil
pinch of sugar
225g/8oz young asparagus spears, trimmed
6 spring onions (scallions), trimmed
salt and ground black pepper
baby spinach leaves, to serve

1 Put the potatoes in a pan. Cover with cold water and bring to the boil. Cook for 10–12 minutes, until tender.

2 Meanwhile, put the broad beans into a bowl. Cut the tomatoes in half and add them to the bowl with the walnuts.

3 Put the white wine vinegar, mustard, olive oil and sugar into a jar. Add salt and pepper to taste. Close the jar tightly and shake well until combined.

4 Add the asparagus to the potatoes and cook for 3 minutes more. Drain the cooked vegetables well, cool under cold running water and drain again. Thickly slice the potatoes. Cut the spring onions into halves.

5 Add the asparagus, potatoes and spring onions to the bowl containing the broad bean mixture. Pour the dressing over the salad and mix until the ingredients are well combined. Serve on a bed of baby spinach leaves.

> **Variations**
> • Use other nuts such as hazelnuts or pecans in place of the walnuts, if you like.
> • Other beans will also work well in this recipe. Try cannellini, butter (lima) or haricot beans instead of the broad beans.

Coronation Salad

The famous salad dressing used in this dish was created especially for the coronation dinner of Queen Elizabeth II. It makes a truly wonderful accompaniment to hard-boiled eggs and potatoes.

Serves 6

450g/1lb new potatoes
45ml/3 tbsp French dressing
3 spring onions (scallions), chopped
6 eggs, hard-boiled and halved
frilly lettuce leaves
¼ cucumber, cut into thin strips
6 large radishes, sliced
1 carton salad cress
salt and ground black pepper

For the coronation dressing
30ml/2 tbsp olive oil
1 small onion, chopped
15ml/1 tbsp mild curry powder or korma spice mix
10ml/2 tsp tomato purée (paste)
30ml/2 tbsp lemon juice
30ml/2 tbsp sherry
300ml/½ pint/1¼ cups mayonnaise
150ml/¼ pint/⅔ cup natural (plain) yogurt

1 Boil the potatoes in salted water until tender. Drain, then transfer to a large bowl and toss them in the French dressing while they are still warm.

2 Stir in the spring onions and the salt and pepper to taste, and allow to cool thoroughly.

3 Meanwhile, make the coronation dressing. Heat the oil in a small pan and fry the onion for 3 minutes, until soft. Stir in the curry powder or spice mix and fry for a further 1 minute. Remove from the heat and mix in the tomato purée, lemon juice, sherry, mayonnaise and yogurt.

4 Stir the dressing into the potatoes, add the eggs, then chill. Line a serving platter with lettuce leaves and pile the salad in the centre. Sprinkle over the cucumber, radishes and cress.

> **Cook's Tip**
> Try making your own mayonnaise and French dressing for this dish, if time allows.

New Spring Salad Energy 323kcal/1343kJ; Protein 5.2g; Carbohydrate 21.5g, of which sugars 2.7g; Fat 24.7g, of which saturates 4g; Cholesterol 88mg; Calcium 49mg; Fibre 2g; Sodium 149mg.
Coronation Salad Energy 587kcal/2429kJ; Protein 10.1g; Carbohydrate 17.1g, of which sugars 4.7g; Fat 51.6g, of which saturates 8.8g; Cholesterol 228mg; Calcium 97mg; Fibre 1.1g; Sodium 401mg.

Hot Cajun Potato Salad

In Cajun country in Louisiana, where Tabasco sauce originates, hot means really hot, so you can go to town with this potato salad if you think you can take it.

Serves 6–8
8 waxy potatoes
1 green (bell) pepper, diced
1 large gherkin, chopped
4 spring onions (scallions), shredded
3 hard-boiled eggs, shelled and chopped
250ml/8fl oz/1 cup mayonnaise
15ml/1 tbsp Dijon mustard
salt and ground black pepper
Tabasco sauce, to taste
pinch or two of cayenne
sliced gherkin, to garnish
mayonnaise, to serve

1 Cook the potatoes in their skins in boiling salted water until tender. Drain and leave to cool.

2 When the potatoes are cool enough to handle, but while they are still warm, peel them and cut into coarse chunks. Place them in a large bowl.

3 Add the green pepper, gherkin, spring onions and hard-boiled eggs to the potatoes and toss gently to combine.

4 In a separate bowl, mix the mayonnaise with the mustard and season with salt, black pepper and Tabasco sauce to taste.

5 Pour the dressing over the potato mixture and toss gently so that the potatoes are well coated. Sprinkle with a pinch or two of cayenne pepper and garnish with a few slices of gherkin. Serve with extra mayonnaise.

Cook's Tips
• The salad is good to eat immediately, when the potatoes are just cool. If you make it in advance and chill it, let it come back to room temperature before serving.
• Tabasco is one of thousands of commercial hot pepper sauces on the market, of varying intensity: use your favourite brand to make this salad.

Curried Potato Salad with Mango Dressing

This sweet and spicy potato salad is a wonderful partner to roasted vegetables.

Serves 4–6
900g/2lb new potatoes
15ml/1 tbsp olive oil
1 onion, sliced into rings
1 garlic clove, crushed
5ml/1 tsp ground cumin
5ml/1 tsp ground coriander
1 mango, peeled, stoned (pitted) and diced
30ml/2 tbsp demerara (raw) sugar
30ml/2 tbsp lime juice
15ml/1 tbsp sesame seeds
salt and ground black pepper
deep fried coriander (cilantro) leaves, to garnish

1 Cut the potatoes in half, then cook them in their skins in boiling salted water until tender. Drain well.

2 Heat the oil in a frying pan (skillet) and fry the onion and garlic over a low heat for 10 minutes until they start to brown.

3 Stir in the ground cumin and coriander and fry for a few seconds. Stir in the mango and sugar and fry for 5 minutes, until soft. Remove the pan from the heat and squeeze in the lime juice. Season with salt and pepper.

4 Place the potatoes in a large bowl and spoon over the mango dressing. Sprinkle with sesame seeds and serve while the dressing is still warm. Garnish the salad with the deep fried coriander leaves.

Cook's Tip
To prepare the mango, cut through the mango lengthwise on either side of the stone (pit) to slice off two sections. Leaving the skin on each section, cross hatch the flesh, then bend it back so that the cubes stand proud of the skin. Slice them off with a small knife. Peel the remaining central section of the mango, then cut off the remaining flesh in chunks and dice.

Cajun Potato Salad Energy 289kcal/1197kJ; Protein 4g; Carbohydrate 10.3g, of which sugars 2.7g; Fat 26.1g, of which saturates 4.2g; Cholesterol 95mg; Calcium 21mg; Fibre 0.9g; Sodium 229mg.
Curried Potato Salad Energy 174kcal/737kJ; Protein 3.3g; Carbohydrate 33.7g, of which sugars 11.2g; Fat 3.8g, of which saturates 0.7g; Cholesterol 0mg; Calcium 34mg; Fibre 2.5g; Sodium 18mg.

Caribbean Potato Salad

Colourful vegetables in a creamy smooth dressing make this piquant potato salad ideal to serve on its own or with a vegetable flan.

Serves 6

900g/2lb small waxy or
  salad potatoes
2 red (bell) peppers, seeded
  and diced
2 celery sticks, finely chopped
1 shallot, finely chopped
2 or 3 spring onions (scallions),
  finely chopped

1 mild fresh green chilli, seeded
  and finely chopped
1 garlic clove, crushed
10ml/2 tsp finely chopped chives
10ml/2 tsp finely chopped basil
15ml/1 tbsp finely chopped
  fresh parsley
15ml/1 tbsp single (light) cream
30ml/2 tbsp salad cream
15ml/1 tbsp mayonnaise
5ml/1 tsp Dijon mustard
7.5ml/1/2 tbsp sugar
chopped chives and chopped
  red chilli, to garnish

1 Cook the potatoes in a large pan of boiling water until tender but still firm. Drain and set aside. When cool enough to handle, cut the potatoes into 2.5cm/1in cubes and place in a large salad bowl.

2 Add the peppers, celery, shallot and spring onions to the potatoes in the salad bowl, together with the chilli, garlic and all the chopped herbs.

3 Mix together the cream, salad cream, mayonnaise, mustard and sugar in a small bowl. Stir well until the mixture is thoroughly combined and forms a smooth dressing.

4 Pour the dressing over the potatoes and stir gently to coat. Serve garnished with chives and chopped red chilli.

> **Variation**
> *To transform this light salad into a more substantial and complete meal, add quartered hard-boiled eggs and cooked green beans, serve on a bed of lettuce and top with sliced black olives.*

Gado Gado Salad with Peanut Sambal

This Indonesian potato salad combines lightly steamed vegetables and hard-boiled eggs with a richly flavoured dressing made from peanut butter and soy sauce.

Serves 6

225g/8oz new potatoes, halved
2 carrots, cut into sticks
115g/4oz green beans
1/2 small cauliflower, broken
  into florets
1/4 firm white cabbage, shredded
200g/7oz bean or lentil sprouts

4 eggs, hard-boiled and quartered
bunch of watercress (optional)

For the sauce
90ml/6 tbsp crunchy
  peanut butter
300ml/1/2 pint/1 1/4 cups
  cold water
1 garlic clove, crushed
30ml/2 tbsp dark soy sauce
15ml/1 tbsp dry sherry
10ml/2 tsp caster
  (superfine) sugar
15ml/1 tbsp fresh lemon juice
5ml/1 tsp anchovy essence (paste)

1 Place the halved potatoes in a metal colander or steamer and set over a pan of gently boiling water. Cover the pan or steamer with a lid and cook the potatoes for 10 minutes.

2 Add the rest of the vegetables to the steamer and steam for a further 10 minutes, until tender. Cool and arrange on a platter with the egg quarters and the watercress, if using.

3 Beat together all the ingredients for the sauce in a large mixing bowl until smooth. Drizzle a little sauce over each salad then pour the rest into a small bowl and serve separately.

> **Variation**
> *There are a whole range of nut butters available in supermarkets and health-food stores. Try using hazelnut, almond or cashew nut butter in place of peanut butter to create a slightly milder flavoured sauce. Alternatively, make your own peanut butter by blending 225g/8oz/2 cups peanuts with 120ml/4fl oz/1/2 cup oil in a food processor.*

Caribbean Potato Salad Energy 176kcal/742kJ; Protein 3.8g; Carbohydrate 31.3g, of which sugars 8.7g; Fat 4.8g, of which saturates 1g; Cholesterol 5mg; Calcium 42mg; Fibre 3.2g; Sodium 92mg.
Gado Gado Salad Energy 199kcal/831kJ; Protein 10.5g; Carbohydrate 14g, of which sugars 6.6g; Fat 11.3g, of which saturates 2.9g; Cholesterol 127mg; Calcium 58mg; Fibre 3.1g; Sodium 819mg.

Cheese and Potato Truffade

Baked until meltingly soft, this warming cheese and potato supper is the perfect slow bake to come home to. In France, where it originated, it would be made with a Tomme or Cantal cheese, which are now readily available.

Serves 4–6

a little sunflower oil or
   melted butter

1 large onion, thinly sliced
675g/1½lb baking potatoes, very
   thinly sliced
150g/5oz/1¼ cups grated hard
   cheese, such as Tomme, Cantal
   or mature (sharp) Cheddar
freshly grated nutmeg
salt and ground black pepper
mixed salad leaves, to serve

1 Preheat the oven to 180°C/350°F/Gas 4. Lightly grease the base of a shallow baking dish or roasting pan with the oil or melted butter.

2 Arrange the onions over the bottom of the dish and then add a layer of potatoes over them, and a sprinkling of cheese. Finish with another layer of potatoes.

3 Brush the top layer of potatoes with oil or melted butter and season with nutmeg, salt and pepper.

4 Top the dish with a layer of the grated cheese. Bake in the preheated oven for about 1 hour until the vegetables are tender and the top is golden brown.

5 Leave the dish to stand for about 5 minutes, then serve in wedges with mixed salad leaves.

Cook's Tips
Slice your potatoes with a mandolin to guarantee that they are beautifully uniform and paper thin. If you do not have access to a mandolin then use a very sharp knife, but take your time and be careful to ensure that you don't cut yourself.

Potatoes Baked with Tomatoes

This simple, hearty dish from the south of Italy is best when potatoes and tomatoes are in season and bursting with flavour, but it can also be made with canned plum tomatoes.

Serves 6

2 large red or yellow onions,
   thinly sliced

1kg/2¼lb baking potatoes,
   thinly sliced
450g/1lb tomatoes, fresh or
   canned, sliced, with their juice
90ml/6 tbsp olive oil
115g/4oz/1 cup Parmesan
   or Cheddar cheese,
   freshly grated
a few fresh basil leaves
50ml/2fl oz/¼ cup water
salt and ground black pepper

1 Preheat the oven to 180°C/350°F/Gas 4. Brush a large baking dish generously with oil.

2 Arrange a layer of onions in the base of the dish, followed by layers of potatoes and tomatoes, alternating them to make the dish look colourful.

3 Pour a little of the olive oil over the surface, and sprinkle with some of the grated cheese. Season with salt and ground black pepper.

4 Continue to layer the vegetables in the dish until they are all used up. Finish with a decorative top layer of overlapping potatoes and tomatoes.

5 Tear the basil leaves into small pieces, and add them here and there among the vegetables, saving a few for garnish. Sprinkle the top with the remaining grated cheese and oil.

6 Pour the water over the dish. Bake in the oven for 1 hour until the vegetables are tender.

7 Check the potato dish towards the end of cooking, and if the top begins to brown too much, place a sheet of foil or baking parchment, or a flat baking tray, on top of the dish. Garnish the dish with the remaining fresh basil leaves, once it is cooked, and serve immediately.

Truffade Energy 117kcal/494kJ; Protein 3.2g; Carbohydrate 20.8g, of which sugars 3.4g; Fat 2.9g, of which saturates 1.7g; Cholesterol 7mg; Calcium 40mg; Fibre 1.6g; Sodium 48mg.
Potatoes with Tomatoes Energy 309kcal/1290kJ; Protein 9.8g; Carbohydrate 31.7g, of which sugars 8g; Fat 16.7g, of which saturates 4.9g; Cholesterol 15mg; Calcium 211mg; Fibre 3.2g; Sodium 189mg.

Courgette and Potato Bake

Cook this delicious potato dish, known as briami in Greece, in early autumn, and the aromas spilling from the kitchen will recall the rich summer tastes and colours just past. In Greece, this would constitute a hearty main meal, with a salad, some olives and cheese.

Serves 4 as a main course; 6 as a first course

675g/1½lb courgettes (zucchini)
450g/1lb potatoes, peeled and
   cut into chunks
1 onion, finely sliced
3 garlic cloves, chopped
1 large red (bell) pepper, seeded
   and cubed
400g/14oz can chopped tomatoes
150ml/¼ pint/⅔ cup extra virgin
   olive oil
150ml/¼ pint/⅔ cup hot water
5ml/1 tsp dried oregano
45ml/3 tbsp chopped fresh flat
   leaf parsley, plus a few extra
   sprigs, to garnish
salt and ground black pepper

1 Preheat the oven to 190°C/375°F/Gas 5. Scrape the courgettes lightly under running water to dislodge any grit and then slice them into thin rounds.

2 Put them in a large baking dish and add the chopped potatoes, onion, garlic, red pepper and tomatoes. Mix well, then stir in the olive oil, hot water and dried oregano.

3 Spread the mixture evenly, then season with salt and ground black pepper. Bake for 30 minutes, then stir in the parsley and a little more water.

4 Return to the oven and cook for 1 hour, increasing the temperature to 200°C/400°F/Gas 6 for the remaining 10–15 minutes, so that the potatoes brown. Serve hot or cold.

Variation
Other vegetables can be used in this dish, if you like. Substitute half the courgettes with aubergine (eggplant), or add in a handful of pitted black olives.

Vegetable Gratin with Indian Spices

Subtly spiced with curry powder, turmeric, coriander and mild chilli powder, this rich potato gratin is substantial enough to serve on its own for lunch or supper. It also makes a good side dish to a larger meal.

Serves 4

175g/6oz celeriac
2 large potatoes, total weight
   about 450g/1lb
2 sweet potatoes, total weight
   about 275g/10oz
15ml/1 tbsp unsalted butter
5ml/1 tsp curry powder
5ml/1 tsp ground turmeric
2.5ml/½ tsp ground coriander
5ml/1 tsp mild chilli powder
3 shallots, chopped
150ml/¼ pint/⅔ cup single
   (light) cream
150ml/¼ pint/⅔ cup milk
salt and ground black pepper
chopped fresh flat leaf parsley,
   to garnish

1 Thinly slice the celeriac, potatoes and sweet potatoes, using a sharp knife or the slicing attachment on a food processor. Immediately place the vegetables in a bowl of cold water to prevent them from discolouring.

2 Preheat the oven to 180°C/350°F/Gas 4. Heat half the butter in a heavy pan, add the curry powder, turmeric and coriander and half of the chilli powder. Cook for 2 minutes, then leave to cool slightly. Drain the vegetables, then pat dry with kitchen paper. Place in a bowl, add the spice mixture and the shallots, and mix well.

3 Arrange the vegetables in a gratin dish, seasoning with salt and pepper between the layers. Mix together the cream and milk, pour the mixture over the vegetables, then sprinkle the remaining chilli powder on top.

4 Cover the dish with baking parchment and bake in the preheated oven for about 45 minutes.

5 Remove the baking parchment, dot the surface of the gratin with the remaining butter and bake for a further 50 minutes, until it is golden and bubbling. Serve immediately, garnished with the chopped fresh parsley.

Courgette Bake Energy 374kcal/1,554kJ; Protein 6.6g; Carbohydrate 28.6g, of which sugars 11.2g; Fat 26.7g, of which saturates 4g; Cholesterol 0mg; Calcium 86mg; Fibre 5.1g; Sodium 29mg.
Vegetable Gratin Energy 268kcal/1129kJ; Protein 5.8g; Carbohydrate 37.7g, of which sugars 9.8g; Fat 11.6g, of which saturates 7.1g; Cholesterol 31mg; Calcium 127mg; Fibre 3.6g; Sodium 117mg.

Layered Vegetable Terrine

A combination of vegetables and herbs layered and baked in a spinach-lined loaf tin. Delicious served hot or warm with a simple leafy salad garnish.

Serves 6

3 red (bell) peppers, halved
450g/1lb waxy potatoes
115g/4oz spinach leaves, trimmed
25g/1oz/2 tbsp butter
pinch grated nutmeg
115g/4oz/1 cup vegetarian
    Cheddar cheese, grated
1 medium courgette (zucchini),
    sliced lengthways and blanched
salt and ground black pepper

1 Preheat the oven to 180°C/350°F/Gas 4. Place the peppers in a roasting pan and roast, cores in place, for 30–45 minutes until charred.

2 Remove the peppers from the oven. Place in a plastic bag to cool. Peel the skins and remove the cores. Halve the potatoes and boil in lightly salted water for 10–15 minutes.

3 Blanch the spinach for a few seconds in boiling water. Drain and pat dry on kitchen paper. Line the base and sides of a 900g/2lb loaf tin (pan), making sure the leaves overlap the edges of the tin slightly.

4 Slice the potatoes thinly and lay one-third of the potatoes over the base, dot with a little of the butter and season with salt, pepper and nutmeg. Sprinkle a little cheese over.

5 Arrange three of the peeled pepper halves on top. Sprinkle a little cheese over and then a layer of courgettes. Lay another one-third of the potatoes on top with the remaining peppers and some more cheese, seasoning as you go. Lay the final layer of potato on top and sprinkle over any remaining cheese. Fold the spinach leaves over. Cover with foil.

6 Place the loaf tin in a roasting pan and pour boiling water around the outside, making sure the water comes halfway up the sides of the tin. Bake in the oven for 45–60 minutes. Remove from the oven and turn the loaf out. Serve sliced with lettuce and tomatoes.

Layered Potato Bake with Cheese

This family-sized potato bake is substantial enough for a main course.

Serves 6

105ml/7 tbsp olive oil
1 large onion, chopped
2 garlic cloves, crushed
5ml/1 tsp crushed dried chillies
130g/4½oz/generous 1 cup
    walnut halves
130g/4½oz/generous ½ cup
    fresh cheese, such as ricotta
105ml/7 tbsp warm water
3 eggs
450g/1lb large potatoes, peeled
butter, for greasing
65g/2½oz/scant ¾ cup pitted
    black olives
4 pimientos, cut into strips
salt

1 Heat 30ml/2 tbsp of the oil in a small pan over a low heat. Add the onion and sauté gently for 5 minutes, until soft. Stir in the garlic and dried chillies and cook for a further 2 minutes.

2 Put the walnuts in a blender or food processor. Blend until smooth, then add the cooked onion mixture, with the cheese and remaining olive oil. Season generously with salt and pour in the warm water. Blend to make a smooth paste. Set aside.

3 Put the eggs in a small pan of cold water. Bring to the boil, then lower the heat to a simmer. Cook for 10 minutes, then cool in a bowl of cold water.

4 Add the potatoes to a pan of salted water and cover. Bring to the boil, then simmer for 10 minutes. Drain and refresh under cold water. Drain again and cut into 1cm/½in slices. Shell the eggs and cut them into slices.

5 Preheat the oven to 180°C/350°F/Gas 4. Lightly grease a 28 × 18cm/11 × 7in baking dish with butter. Arrange a layer of potatoes in the dish and generously spread with the prepared paste. Top with egg slices and a sprinkling of olives and pimiento strips. Continue layering until all the ingredients have been used, finishing with olives and pimientos.

6 Bake for 30 minutes, until the potatoes are very tender. Leave to cool for 5 minutes before serving.

Layered Terrine Energy 205kcal/854kJ; Protein 8.3g; Carbohydrate 19.2g, of which sugars 7.7g; Fat 10.6g, of which saturates 6.6g; Cholesterol 27mg; Calcium 196mg; Fibre 3g; Sodium 203mg.
Layered Bake Energy 572kcal/2363kJ; Protein 8.9g; Carbohydrate 16.7g, of which sugars 4.3g; Fat 52.7g, of which saturates 12.3g; Cholesterol 117mg; Calcium 75mg; Fibre 2.2g; Sodium 116mg.

Potato and Parsnip Amandine

Shells of baked potatoes are filled with a spicy parsnip and crunchy almond mix. They make an unusual and delicious alternative to plain jacket potatoes.

Serves 4
4 large baking potatoes
olive oil, for greasing
225g/8oz parsnips, diced
25g/1oz/2 tbsp butter
5ml/1 tsp cumin seeds
5ml/1 tsp ground coriander
30ml/2 tbsp single (light) cream
  or natural (plain) yogurt
salt and ground black pepper
115g/4oz Gruyère or Cheddar
  cheese, grated
1 egg, beaten
50g/2oz/1/4 cup flaked
  (sliced) almonds

1 Preheat the oven to 200°C/400°F/Gas 6. Rub the potatoes all over with the olive oil, score each lightly around its width, then bake in the oven for about 1 hour, until cooked.

2 Meanwhile, boil the parsnips until tender, then drain well, mash them and mix with the butter, spices and cream or natural yogurt.

3 When the potatoes are cooked, leave them to cool slightly, then cut them in half and scoop out the flesh with a spoon. Mash the flesh, then combine with the parsnip mash and season well with salt and black pepper.

4 Stir the cheese, egg and three-quarters of the almonds into the potato and parsnip mash. Fill the hollow potato shells with the mixture and sprinkle over the remaining almonds.

5 Return the filled potatoes to the oven and bake for about 15–20 minutes until golden brown and the filling has set lightly. Serve immediately with a side salad.

> **Cook's Tip**
> This dish works just as well with single (light) cream or natural (plain) yogurt. Which one you use is a matter of preference and may be influenced by the kind of diet you tend to follow.

Baked Scalloped Potatoes with Feta

Thinly sliced potatoes are cooked with Greek feta cheese and black and green olives in olive oil. This dish is a good one to serve with toasted pitta bread.

Serves 4
900g/2lb maincrop potatoes
150ml/1/4 pint/2/3 cup olive oil
1 sprig rosemary
275g/10oz/2 1/2 cups feta
  cheese, crumbled
115g/4oz/1 cup pitted black
  and green olives, halved
300ml/1/2 pint/1 1/4 cups hot
  vegetable stock
salt and ground black pepper

1 Preheat the oven to 200°C/400°F/Gas 6. Cook the potatoes in plenty of boiling water for 15 minutes. Drain and cool slightly.

2 When the potatoes are cool enough to handle, peel them and cut into thin slices.

3 Lightly grease the base and sides of a 1.5 litre/2 1/2 pint/6 1/4 cup rectangular ovenproof dish with a little of the olive oil.

4 Layer the potatoes in the base of the dish. Break up the rosemary sprig and sprinkle over the potatoes along with the feta cheese and olives.

5 Drizzle with the remaining olive oil and pour over the stock. Season with salt and plenty of ground black pepper.

6 Bake in the oven for about 35 minutes, covering with foil to prevent the potatoes from getting too brown. Serve hot, straight from the dish.

> **Cook's Tips**
> • Make sure you choose good-quality Greek feta cheese, which has a different texture to the feta cheese that is produced in other countries.
> • Try to find fresh olives for this dish, which should be available from the deli counter of your local supermarket, as olives that are canned in brine will be too salty for this dish.

Potato Amandine Energy 452kcal/1888kJ; Protein 16.2g; Carbohydrate 40.4g, of which sugars 6.7g; Fat 25.5g, of which saturates 11.8g; Cholesterol 94mg; Calcium 293mg; Fibre 5.5g; Sodium 305mg.
Scalloped Potatoes Energy 584kcal/2429kJ; Protein 14.8g; Carbohydrate 37.3g, of which sugars 4g; Fat 42.7g, of which saturates 13.7g; Cholesterol 48mg; Calcium 279mg; Fibre 3.1g; Sodium 1662mg.

Cowboy's Vegetable Hotpot

A great dish to serve as a children's main meal, which adults will enjoy too – if they are allowed to join the posse. You can use any vegetable mixture you like – just remember that potatoes and baked beans are a must for every self-respecting cowboy.

Serves 4–6
45ml/3 tbsp sunflower oil
1 onion, sliced
1 red (bell) pepper, sliced
1 sweet potato or 2 carrots, cut into chunks
115g/4oz green beans, chopped
1 x 400g/14oz can baked beans
1 x 200g/7oz can corn
15ml/1 tbsp tomato purée (paste)
5ml/1 tsp barbecue spice seasoning
115g/4oz cheese (preferably smoked), cubed
450g/1lb potatoes, thinly sliced
25g/1oz/2 tbsp butter, melted
salt and ground black pepper

1 Heat the sunflower oil in a large, heavy frying pan. Add the sliced onion, red pepper and sweet potato or carrots to the frying pan and cook gently for about 5 minutes, until softened but not browned.

2 Add the green beans, baked beans, corn (including the liquid from the can of corn), tomato purée and barbecue spice seasoning. Stir well to combine all of the ingredients and then bring the mixture to a boil. Reduce the heat and simmer gently for about 10 minutes.

3 Transfer the vegetables to a shallow ovenproof dish, spreading them out into an even layer. Sprinkle the cubed cheese over the top of the vegetables.

4 Preheat the oven to 190°C/375°F/Gas 5. Layer the sliced potatoes over the vegetable and cheese mixture and brush with the melted butter. Season generously with salt and ground black pepper.

5 Place the hotpot in the preheated oven and bake for about 30–40 minutes until it is golden brown on top and the potato slices are just tender. Serve immediately.

Three Vegetable Kugel

Grated seasonal vegetables are baked until crisp on top and creamy and tender inside. This version of the classic Jewish casserole combines the traditional flavours and method but uses a more contemporary combination of vegetables.

Serves 4
2 courgettes (zucchini), coarsely grated
2 carrots, coarsely grated
2 potatoes, peeled and coarsely grated
1 onion, grated
3 eggs, lightly beaten
3 garlic cloves, chopped
pinch of sugar
15ml/1 tbsp finely chopped fresh parsley
2–3 pinches of dried basil
30–45ml/2–3 tbsp matzo meal
105ml/7 tbsp olive oil or vegetable oil
salt and ground black pepper

1 Preheat the oven to 180°C/350°F/Gas 4. Put the courgettes, carrots, potatoes, onion, eggs, garlic, sugar, parsley, basil, salt and pepper in a bowl and combine.

2 Add the matzo meal to the bowl and stir together until the mixture forms a thick batter.

3 Pour half the olive or vegetable oil into an ovenproof dish. Spoon in the vegetable mixture, then evenly pour over the remaining oil.

4 Bake in the preheated oven for 40–60 minutes, or until the vegetables are tender and the kugel top is golden brown. Serve immediately.

> **Cook's Tip**
> Matzo is a brittle unleavened bread, rather like a cracker. It is made with plain (all-purpose) flour and water, although some have additional flavourings, such as onion. Matzo is traditionally eaten during the Jewish Passover festival in place of leavened bread, which cannot be eaten at that time. Matzo meal is made by grinding matzos, and comes in fine or medium texture.

Cowboy Hotpot pot Energy 351kcal/1470kJ; Protein 12g; Carbohydrate 40.1g, of which sugars 11.1g; Fat 16.6g, of which saturates 7.3g; Cholesterol 27mg; Calcium 199mg; Fibre 5.7g; Sodium 503mg.
Vegetable Kugel Energy 358kcal/1488kJ; Protein 9.2g; Carbohydrate 26.6g, of which sugars 5.7g; Fat 24.5g, of which saturates 4.2g; Cholesterol 143mg; Calcium 63mg; Fibre 2.9g; Sodium 71mg.

Grated Potato Casserole

This recipe comes from Satakunta, a south-western region of Finland. Floury, maincrop potatoes will produce the best results.

Serves 4
a small knob (pat) of butter
2 eggs
250ml/8floz/1 cup full-fat (whole) milk
30ml/2 tbsp plain (all-purpose) flour
5ml/1 tsp salt
2 potatoes
15ml/1 tbsp chopped fresh parsley, to garnish (optional)

1 Preheat the oven to 180°C/350°F/Gas 4. Melt the butter gently in a pan and use it to grease an ovenproof dish.

2 Beat the eggs together in a large mixing bowl, then add the milk and mix together.

3 Add the flour and salt to the eggs and milk and mix with your hands until the mixture forms a smooth batter.

4 Peel the potatoes, then grate them using a hand grater and add them to the batter.

5 Transfer the potato mixture to the prepared dish, then bake in the oven for about 50 minutes, until the potatoes are cooked. Serve hot, sprinkled with chopped parsley, if using.

Cook's Tip
Fresh parsley is simple to grow yourself. Buy a plant and keep it on a sunny windowsill in your kitchen. Ensure it is kept moist but don't over-water it and pull off the leaves as and when you need them. They will regrow in a matter of days.

Variation
To make a richer, creamier version, substitute half the milk with single (light) cream.

Casserole with Harvest Vegetables

In autumn, thoughts turn to hearty, satisfying food. This sustaining, yet low-fat dish is the ideal choice.

Serves 6
15ml/1 tbsp sunflower oil
2 leeks, sliced
1 garlic clove, crushed
4 celery sticks, chopped
2 carrots, sliced
2 parsnips, diced
1 sweet potato, diced
225g/8oz swede (rutabaga), diced
175g/6oz/¾ cup whole brown or green lentils
450g/1lb tomatoes, peeled, seeded and chopped
15ml/1 tbsp chopped fresh thyme
15ml/1 tbsp chopped fresh marjoram
900ml/1½ pints/3¾ cups vegetable stock
15ml/1 tbsp cornflour (cornstarch)
45ml/3 tbsp water
salt and ground black pepper
fresh thyme sprigs, to garnish

1 Preheat the oven to 180°C/350°F/Gas 4. Heat the oil in a large, flameproof casserole. Add the leeks, garlic and celery and cook over a low heat, stirring occasionally, for 3 minutes, until the leeks begin to soften.

2 Add the carrots, parsnips, sweet potato, swede, lentils, tomatoes, herbs and stock. Stir well and season with salt and ground black pepper to taste. Bring to the boil, stirring the mixture occasionally.

3 Cover the casserole, put it in the oven and bake for about 50 minutes, until the vegetables and lentils are tender, stirring the vegetable mixture once or twice.

4 Remove the casserole from the oven. Blend the cornflour with the water in a small bowl until it forms a smooth paste.

5 Stir the cornflour mixture into the casserole and heat it gently on top of the stove, stirring constantly, until the mixture boils and thickens. Lower the heat and simmer gently for 2 minutes, stirring.

6 Spoon on to warmed serving plates or into bowls, garnish with the thyme sprigs and serve.

Grated Potato Casserole Energy 215kcal/894kJ; Protein 8.7g; Carbohydrate 13g, of which sugars 3.3g; Fat 14.7g, of which saturates 7.7g; Cholesterol 123mg; Calcium 277mg; Fibre 3g; Sodium 297mg.
Harvest Casserole Energy 202kcal/857kJ; Protein 9.4g; Carbohydrate 36.2g, of which sugars 10.3g; Fat 3.2g, of which saturates 0.5g; Cholesterol 0mg; Calcium 70mg; Fibre 6.4g; Sodium 60mg.

Winter Vegetable Hotpot

Making this in the microwave and then finishing it under a grill results in a richly flavoured and substantial one-pot meal. To accompany the potatoes in this recipe, use whatever other seasonal vegetables you have to hand.

Serves 4

2 onions, sliced
4 carrots, sliced
1 small swede (rutabaga), sliced
2 parsnips, sliced
3 small turnips, sliced
1/2 celeriac, cut into matchsticks
2 leeks, thinly sliced
1 garlic clove, chopped
1 bay leaf, crumbled
30ml/2 tbsp chopped fresh mixed
   herbs, such as parsley
   and thyme
300ml/1/2 pint/1 1/4 cups
   vegetable stock
15ml/1 tbsp plain
   (all-purpose) flour
675g/1 1/2lb red-skinned potatoes,
   scrubbed and thinly sliced
50g/2oz/4 tbsp butter
salt and ground black pepper

1 Arrange all the vegetables, except the potatoes, in layers in a large microwave-proof dish with a tight-fitting lid.

2 Season the vegetable layers lightly with salt and pepper, and sprinkle them with chopped garlic, crumbled bay leaf and chopped herbs.

3 Blend the stock into the flour and pour over the vegetables. Carefully arrange the potatoes in overlapping layers on top. Dot with butter and cover tightly.

4 Microwave on HIGH for 10 minutes. Reduce the power setting to MEDIUM and microwave for a further 25–30 minutes or until the vegetables are tender. Remove the lid and cook under a preheated hot grill (broiler) until the potato top is golden and crisp. Serve hot.

> **Cook's Tip**
> *This recipe is also suitable for cooking in a combination microwave. Follow the oven manufacturer's timing guide for the best results.*

Mixed-bean and Potato Hotpot

This slow-cooker dish, topped with sliced potatoes, is incredibly easy, making the most of dried and canned ingredients from the kitchen.

Serves 6

40g/1 1/2oz/3 tbsp butter
4 shallots, peeled and
   finely chopped
40g/1 1/2oz/1/3 cup plain
   (all-purpose) or wholemeal
   (whole-wheat) flour
300ml/1/2 pint/1 1/4 cups passata
   (bottled strained tomatoes)
120ml/4fl oz/1/2 cup unsweetened
   apple juice
60ml/4 tbsp soft light brown sugar
60ml/4 tbsp tomato ketchup
60ml/4 tbsp dry sherry
60ml/4 tbsp cider vinegar
60ml/4 tbsp light soy sauce
400g/14oz can butter (lima) beans
400g/14oz can flageolet (small
   cannellini) beans
400g/14oz can chickpeas
175g/6oz green beans, cut into
   2.5cm/1in lengths
225g/8oz/3 cups mushrooms, sliced
450g/1lb unpeeled potatoes,
   thinly sliced
15ml/1 tbsp olive oil
15ml/1 tbsp chopped fresh thyme
15ml/1 tbsp fresh marjoram
salt and ground black pepper
fresh herbs, to garnish

1 Melt the butter in a pan, add the shallots and fry gently for 5–6 minutes, until soft. Add the flour and cook for 1 minute, stirring, then gradually stir in the passata. Add the apple juice, sugar, tomato ketchup, sherry, vinegar and light soy sauce to the pan and stir in. Bring to the boil, stirring constantly until it thickens.

2 Rinse the beans and chickpeas and drain. Place them in the slow cooker pot with the green beans and mushrooms and pour in the sauce. Stir, then cover and cook on high for 3 hours.

3 Meanwhile, par-boil the potatoes for 4 minutes. Drain well, then toss them in the oil so that they are lightly coated all over.

4 Stir the herbs into the vegetable mixture and season. Arrange the potato slices on top, overlapping them slightly so that they completely cover them. Cover the pot and cook for a further 2 hours, or until the potatoes are tender.

5 Place the cooking pot under a medium grill (broiler) and cook for 4–5 minutes to brown. Serve garnished with herbs.

Bean Hotpot Energy 483kcal/2042kJ; Protein 18.5g; Carbohydrate 73.3g, of which sugars 24.8g; Fat 13.8g, of which saturates 4.5g; Cholesterol 14mg; Calcium 134mg; Fibre 10.9g; Sodium 826mg.
Winter Hotpot Energy 367kcal/1542kJ; Protein 8.5g; Carbohydrate 58.2g, of which sugars 24.5g; Fat 12.8g, of which saturates 7g; Cholesterol 27mg; Calcium 203mg; Fibre 13.1g; Sodium 178mg.

Middle-eastern Vegetable Stew

A spiced dish of mixed vegetables makes a delicious and filling vegetarian main course in this microwave recipe. Children may prefer less chilli.

Serves 4–6
45ml/3 tbsp vegetable stock
1 green (bell) pepper, seeded
   and sliced
2 courgettes (zucchini), sliced
2 carrots, sliced
2 celery sticks, sliced
2 potatoes, diced
400g/14oz can chopped tomatoes
5ml/1 tsp chilli powder
30ml/2 tbsp chopped fresh mint
400g/14oz can chickpeas, drained
15ml/1 tbsp ground cumin
salt and ground black pepper
mint sprigs, to garnish

1 Place the vegetable stock in a large microwave-proof casserole with the sliced pepper, courgettes, carrots and celery. Cover and microwave on HIGH for 2 minutes.

2 Add the potatoes, tomatoes, chilli powder, fresh mint, chickpeas and ground cumin to the vegetable dish and stir well. Cover the dish and microwave on HIGH for 15–20 minutes, remembering to stir twice during the cooking time.

3 Leave to stand, covered, for 5 minutes, until all the vegetables are tender. Season to taste with salt and pepper and serve hot, garnished with mint leaves.

Cook's Tip
Chickpeas are a traditional ingredient in this type of Middle-Eastern dish. If you prefer, you can use dried ones rather than canned. They will need soaking for a few hours, or overnight, before being boiled until tender.

Variation
Other vegetables can be substituted for those in the recipe, just use whatever you have to hand – try swede (rutabaga), sweet potato or parsnips.

Braised Barley and Vegetables

One of the oldest of cultivated cereals, pot barley has a nutty flavour and slightly chewy texture. It makes a warming and filling dish when combined with root vegetables.

Serves 4
225g/8oz/1 cup pearl or
   pot barley
30ml/2 tbsp sunflower oil
1 large onion, chopped
2 celery sticks, sliced
2 carrots, halved lengthways
   and sliced
225g/8oz swede (rutabaga)
   or turnip, cut into
   2cm/3/4in cubes
225g/8oz potatoes, cut into
   2cm/3/4in cubes
475ml/16fl oz/2 cups
   vegetable stock
salt and ground black pepper
celery leaves, to garnish

1 Put the pearl or pot barley in a measuring jug (cup) and add enough cold water to reach the 600ml/1 pint/2½ cup mark. Leave to soak in a cool place for at least 4 hours, or overnight if time permits.

2 Heat the oil in a large frying pan or flameproof casserole and fry the onion for about 5 minutes until beginning to soften.

3 Add the sliced celery and carrots to the pan and cook, stirring occasionally, for 3–4 minutes, or until the onion is starting to brown.

4 Add the barley and its soaking liquid to the pan. Then add the swede or turnip, potato and stock to the barley, stirring to ensure the ingredients are well combined. Season with salt and ground black pepper.

5 Bring the mixture slowly to the boil, then reduce the heat and cover the pan with a tight-fitting lid.

6 Simmer for about 40 minutes, or until most of the stock has been absorbed and the barley is tender. Stir the mixture occasionally towards the end of the cooking time to prevent the barley from sticking to the base of the pan. Serve, garnished with celery leaves.

Middle-Eastern Stew Energy 149kcal/630kJ; Protein 7.8g; Carbohydrate 24.9g, of which sugars 6.8g; Fat 2.7g, of which saturates 0.4g; Cholesterol 0mg; Calcium 66mg; Fibre 5.7g; Sodium 172mg.
Braised Vegetables Energy 333kcal/1407kJ; Protein 6.6g; Carbohydrate 65g, of which sugars 8.3g; Fat 7g, of which saturates 0.8g; Cholesterol 0mg; Calcium 69mg; Fibre 3.1g; Sodium 33mg.

Potato, Leek and Apple Pie

Apples are the unusual ingredient used to flavour this warming potato dish. A perfect meal on a cold winter evening.

Serves 6
1.5kg/3lb potatoes
3 leeks, sliced
60ml/4 tbsp olive oil
3 onions, roughly chopped
small head of celery, chopped
2 large cooking apples
50g/2oz potato flour or cornflour (cornstarch)
450ml/¾ pint/scant 2 cups milk or soya milk
75g/3oz pumpkin seeds, partially pulverized in a food processor
15ml/1 tbsp sesame seeds
salt and ground black pepper

1 Preheat the oven to 180°C/350°F/Gas 4. Scrub the potatoes or sweet potatoes well and cut into thin slices. Par-cook them, with the leeks, in a steamer or microwave for about 10 minutes or until softened.

2 Lightly grease a shallow, ovenproof dish. Arrange half of the potatoes and all of the leeks in a layer at the base of the dish.

3 Peel, core and dice the apples. Heat 45ml/3 tbsp of the oil in a pan and cook the onions, celery and apples until soft.

4 Add the potato or cornflour, stir well, then add the milk and continue to cook until the sauce thickens. Spoon over the potatoes and leeks, then cover with the remaining potato slices.

5 Brush the top of the potatoes with the remaining 15ml/1 tbsp oil. Season, then sprinkle over the pumpkin and sesame seeds.

6 Bake for 20–30 minutes or until the dish is well heated through and the potatoes on top are lightly browned. Serve immediately.

Cook's Tip
If you have trouble slicing the potatoes or sweet potatoes, cook them whole and slice them when cooked.

Shepherdess Pie

A no-meat version of the timeless potato-topped classic, this dish also has no dairy products in it, so it is suitable for those on a vegan diet. However, you can serve it with confidence to anyone wanting a hearty and delicious meal.

Serves 6–8
1kg/2lb potatoes
45ml/3 tbsp extra virgin olive oil
salt and ground black pepper
1 large onion, chopped
1 green (bell) pepper, chopped
2 carrots, coarsely grated
2 garlic cloves
45ml/3 tbsp sunflower oil or margarine
115g/4oz mushrooms, chopped
2 x 400g/14oz cans aduki beans, drained
600ml/1 pint/2½ cups stock
5ml/1 tsp vegetable yeast extract
2 bay leaves
5ml/1 tsp dried mixed herbs
dried breadcrumbs or chopped nuts, to sprinkle

1 Put the potatoes in a large pan. Add water to cover and bring to the boil. Add salt, then simmer for about 15 minutes, or until the potatoes are tender, but do not let them get too soft. Drain thoroughly and leave to cool.

2 Peel the potatoes (potatoes are easier to peel when boiled in their skins. This also helps preserve more of the vitamins). Mash the peeled potatoes well, mixing in the olive oil and seasoning until you have a smooth purée.

3 In a frying pan, gently fry the onion, pepper, carrots and garlic in the sunflower oil or margarine for about 5–7 minutes until they are soft.

4 Stir in the mushrooms and beans and cook for a further 2 minutes, then add the stock, yeast extract, bay leaves and mixed herbs. Simmer for 15 minutes. Meanwhile, preheat the grill (broiler).

5 Remove the bay leaves and empty the vegetables into a shallow ovenproof dish. Spoon on the potatoes in dollops and sprinkle over the crumbs or nuts. Cook under the grill until golden brown. Serve immediately.

Potato and Apple Pie Energy 446kcal/1837kJ; Protein 12.4g; Carbohydrate 69.1g, of which sugars 16.2g; Fat 15.1g, of which saturates 7.1g; Cholesterol 118mg; Calcium 58mg; Fibre 6.6g; Sodium 69.7mg.
Shepherdess Pie Energy 305kcal/1285kJ; Protein 11.9g; Carbohydrate 46.7g, of which sugars 7.6g; Fat 9.1g, of which saturates 1.3g; Cholesterol 0mg; Calcium 63mg; Fibre 7.7g; Sodium 74mg.

Potato and Leek Filo Pie

This filo pastry pie makes an attractive and unusual centrepiece for a vegetarian buffet. Serve it cool, with a choice of salads.

Serves 8
800g/1¾lb new potatoes, sliced
75g/3oz/6 tbsp butter
400g/14oz leeks, thinly sliced
15g/½oz parsley, finely chopped
60ml/4 tbsp chopped mixed fresh herbs (such as chervil, chives, a little tarragon and basil)
12 sheets filo pastry
150g/5oz Cheshire, Lancashire or Cantal cheese, sliced
2 garlic cloves, finely chopped
250ml/8floz/1 cup double (heavy) cream
2 large egg yolks
salt and ground black pepper

1 Preheat the oven to 190°C/375°F/Gas 5. Cook the potatoes in boiling, salted water for 3–4 minutes. Drain and set aside.

2 Melt 25g/1oz/2 tbsp of the butter in a frying pan and fry the leeks gently, stirring, until softened. Remove from the heat, season and stir in half the parsley and half the mixed herbs.

3 Melt the remaining butter. Line a 23cm/9in loose-based metal cake tin (pan) with 6–7 sheets of filo pastry, brushing each layer with butter. Let the edges overhang the tin. Layer the potatoes, leeks and cheese in the tin, sprinkling a few herbs and the garlic between the layers. Season.

4 Flip the overhanging pastry over the filling and cover with two sheets of filo, tucking in the sides to fit and brushing with melted butter as before. Cover the pie loosely with foil and bake for 35 minutes. (Keep the remaining pastry covered.)

5 Meanwhile, beat the cream, egg yolks and remaining herbs together. Make a hole in the centre of the pie and gradually pour in the eggs and cream.

6 Arrange the remaining pastry on top, teasing it into swirls and folds, then brush with melted butter. Reduce the oven temperature to 180°C/350°F/Gas 4 and bake the pie for another 25–30 minutes, until the top is golden and crisp. Allow to cool before serving.

Vegetarian Moussaka

This tasty dish of layered aubergines, potatoes and courgettes is ideal for a dinner party as it can be made ahead of time, and then reheated when needed.

Serves 8
150ml/¼ pint/⅔ cup olive oil, plus extra if required
2 large aubergines (eggplants), thinly sliced
6 courgettes (zucchini), diced
675g/1½lb potatoes, thinly sliced
2 onions, sliced
3 garlic cloves, crushed
150ml/¼ pint/⅔ cup white wine
2 x 400g/14oz cans chopped tomatoes
30ml/2 tbsp tomato purée (paste)
1 x 430g/15oz can green lentils
10ml/2 tsp dried oregano
60ml/4 tbsp fresh parsley, chopped
225g/8oz/2 cups feta cheese, diced
salt and ground black pepper

For the béchamel sauce
40g/1½oz/3 tbsp butter
40g/1½oz/4 tbsp plain (all-purpose) flour
600ml/1 pint/2½ cups milk
2 eggs, beaten
115g/4oz Parmesan cheese
nutmeg, freshly grated

1 Heat the oil in a frying pan and cook the aubergines and courgettes. Drain on a kitchen paper towel. Brown the potato slices, remove and pat dry. Add the onion and garlic to the pan with a little extra oil, if required, and cook until softened.

2 Pour in the wine and cook until reduced down, then add the tomatoes and lentils plus the liquid from the can. Stir in the herbs and season well. Cover and simmer for 15 minutes.

3 In an ovenproof dish, layer the vegetables, adding the sauce in between and sprinkling with feta. Top with a layer of aubergine. Cover with foil and bake at 190°C/375°F/Gas 5 for 25 minutes.

4 Meanwhile, for the béchamel sauce, put the butter, flour and milk into a pan all together and bring slowly to a boil, stirring until thickened and smooth. Season and add the nutmeg. Remove the sauce from the heat, then beat in the eggs. Pour over the aubergines and sprinkle with the Parmesan.

5 To finish, return to the oven, uncovered, and bake for a further 25–30 minutes until golden and bubbling hot.

Potato and Leek Pie Energy 468kcal/1948kJ; Protein 10.7g; Carbohydrate 33g, of which sugars 3.5g; Fat 33.1g, of which saturates 20g; Cholesterol 137mg; Calcium 225mg; Fibre 3.2g; Sodium 218mg.
Moussaka Energy 588kcal/2445kJ; Protein 37.9g; Carbohydrate 14.8g, of which sugars 3.7g; Fat 40.9g, of which saturates 18.2g; Cholesterol 206mg; Calcium 379mg; Fibre 2.4g; Sodium 506mg.

Grilled Vegetables with Bagna Cauda

Bagna cauda means 'warm bath' and this rich dip is the traditional Piedmontese accompaniment to raw or cooked vegetables. It is kept warm in an earthenware dish over a candle heater, but the edge of a waning barbecue is also ideal.

Serves 4–6
675g/1½lb sweet potatoes
375g/13oz carrots
400g/14oz parsnips
400g/14oz raw beetroot (beets)
450g/1lb asparagus, trimmed
60ml/4 tbsp extra virgin olive oil
salt and ground black pepper

For the bagna cauda
3–4 garlic cloves, crushed
50–65g/2–2½oz drained capers, chopped
25g/1oz/2 tbsp unsalted butter, melted
200ml/7fl oz/scant 1 cup extra virgin olive oil

1 Prepare the barbecue. Cutting lengthways, slice each sweet potato and carrot into eight pieces, each parsnip into seven and each beetroot into ten. Toss all the vegetables except the beetroot in most of the oil on a big tray. Put the beetroot on a separate tray as it might otherwise stain the other vegetables. Gently toss the beetroot in the remaining oil and season all the vegetables well.

2 Make the bagna cauda. Place the garlic, capers and butter, with a little pepper, into a food processor. Pour in 30ml/2 tbsp of the oil and whizz to a purée. With the motor running, add the remaining oil. Transfer into a heatproof bowl or pan and warm very gently at the edge of the barbecue, or over a pan of simmering water, when ready to serve.

3 Once the flames have died down, position a lightly oiled grill rack over the coals to heat. When the coals are medium-hot, or with a moderate coating of ash, arrange the vegetables over the grill rack.

4 Lightly grill the vegetables for about 3 minutes on each side, or until tender and branded with dark golden grill lines. Remove them as they cook and serve hot or warm with the heated bagna cauda.

Polish Potato Pierogi

These Polish dumplings of spicy mashed potato, served with melted butter and sour cream, are hearty enough to ward off the rigours of a cold winter.

Serves 4–6
675g/1½lb baking potatoes, peeled and cut into chunks
50–75g/2–3oz/4–5 tbsp unsalted butter, plus extra melted butter to serve
3 onions, finely chopped
2 eggs, lightly beaten
1 250g/9oz packet wonton wrappers
salt and ground black pepper
chopped parsley, to garnish
sour cream, to serve

1 Cook the potatoes in a large pan of salted boiling water until tender. Drain well. Meanwhile, melt the butter in a frying pan, add the onions and fry over a medium heat for about 10 minutes, or until browned.

2 Mash the potatoes, then stir in the fried onions and leave them to cool. When cool, add the eggs and mix together. Season with salt and pepper to taste.

3 Brush the edges of the wonton wrappers with a little water. Place 15–30ml/1–2 tbsp of the potato filling in the centre of each wrapper, then top with another sheet. Press the edges together and pinch with your fingers. Set aside to allow the edges to dry out and seal firmly.

4 Bring a pan of salted water to the boil, then lower the heat to a simmer. Carefully slip the dumplings into the water, keeping it simmering gently, and cook for about 2 minutes, until tender.

5 Using a slotted spoon, remove the potato dumplings from the water and drain. Serve the dumplings on plates or in bowls. Drizzle with butter and sour cream and garnish with parsley.

> **Variation**
> Add a generous sprinkling of chopped spring onions (scallions) to the filling.

Grilled Vegetables Energy 571kcal/2378kJ; Protein 8.9g; Carbohydrate 44.9g, of which sugars 21g; Fat 40.9g, of which saturates 7.4g; Cholesterol 10mg; Calcium 131mg; Fibre 10.1g; Sodium 471mg.
Polish Dumplings Energy 364kcal/1532kJ; Protein 10.3g; Carbohydrate 55.9g, of which sugars 7.9g; Fat 12.7g, of which saturates 5.9g; Cholesterol 94mg; Calcium 55mg; Fibre 3.7g; Sodium 164mg.

Bavarian Potato Dumplings

The cuisines of Germany and Central Europe are unimaginable without potato dumplings, consumed in all shapes and sizes. In this version, crunchy croûtons are placed in the centre.

Serves 6

1.5kg/3lb potatoes, peeled
115g/4oz/²/₃ cup semolina
115g/4oz/1 cup wholemeal (whole-wheat) flour
5ml/1 tsp salt
1.5ml/¼ tsp nutmeg
30ml/2 tbsp sunflower oil
2 thin white bread slices, crusts removed, cubed
1.5 litres/2½ pints/6¼ cups vegetable stock
ground black pepper
chopped fresh flat leaf parsley and onion slices, to garnish
melted butter, to serve

1 Put the potatoes in a large pan. Add water to cover and bring to the boil. Add salt, then simmer for about 15 minutes, or until the potatoes are tender.

2 Drain well, mash roughly with a potato masher and then press through a sieve (strainer) with a large spoon into a bowl. Add the semolina, flour, salt, a little pepper and the nutmeg, and mix well.

3 Heat the oil in a heavy frying pan and fry the cubes of bread, stirring frequently, until light golden brown. Drain the croûtons on kitchen paper.

4 Divide the potato mixture into 24 balls. Press a few of the fried croûtons firmly into each dumpling.

5 Bring the vegetable stock to the boil in a large pan, add the dumplings, in batches if necessary, and cook gently for 5 minutes, turning once.

6 Remove the dumplings from the pan with a slotted spoon and arrange on a warmed serving dish. Keep warm while you finish cooking the remainder if cooking in batches. Sprinkle with chopped parsley and fried onion slices and serve with a warmed sauce boat of melted butter.

Spiced Stuffed Vegetables

The vegetarian filling of these oven-roasted vegetables is mildly spiced and has the delicious tang of lemon juice. They are also excellent cold and are good served as an appetizer as well as a main course.

Serves 4

4 potatoes, peeled
4 onions, skinned
4 courgettes (zucchini), halved widthways
2–4 garlic cloves, chopped
45–60ml/3–4 tbsp olive oil
45–60ml/3–4 tbsp tomato purée (paste)
1.5ml/¼ tsp ras al hanout or curry powder
large pinch of ground allspice
seeds of 2–3 cardamom pods
juice of ½ lemon
30–45ml/2–3 tbsp chopped fresh parsley
90–120ml/6–8 tbsp vegetable stock
salt and ground black pepper
salad, to serve (optional)

1 Bring a large pan of salted water to the boil. Starting with the potatoes, then the onions and finally the courgettes, add to the boiling water and cook until they become almost tender but not cooked through. Allow about 10 minutes for the potatoes, 8 minutes for the onions and 4–6 minutes for the courgettes. Remove the vegetables from the pan and set aside to cool.

2 When the vegetables are cool enough to handle, hollow them out using a knife and spoon. Preheat the oven to 190°C/375°F/Gas 5.

3 Finely chop the cut-out vegetable flesh and put it in a bowl. Add the garlic, half of the olive oil, the tomato purée, ras al hanout or curry powder, allspice, cardamom seeds, lemon juice, chopped parsley, salt and pepper, and mix until thoroughly combined. Spoon the stuffing mixture into the hollowed vegetables, filling to just over the top.

4 Arrange the stuffed vegetables in a roasting pan and drizzle with the vegetable stock and the remaining oil. Roast for about 35–40 minutes, or until they are golden brown. Serve warm with a salad, if you like.

Bavarian Dumplings Energy 356kcal/1509kJ; Protein 9.5g; Carbohydrate 71.8g, of which sugars 3.9g; Fat 5.4g, of which saturates 0.8g; Cholesterol 0mg; Calcium 36mg; Fibre 4.8g; Sodium 405mg.
Stuffed Vegetables Energy 347kcal/1452kJ; Protein 10.2g; Carbohydrate 56.7g, of which sugars 22.1g; Fat 10.3g, of which saturates 1.6g; Cholesterol 0mg; Calcium 135mg; Fibre 8.2g; Sodium 62mg.

Potato, Cabbage and Cheddar Cheese Rissoles

Originally made on Mondays with leftover potatoes and cabbage from the Sunday lunch, these rissoles are quick to make and great for any light meal. Make them for brunch teamed with fried eggs, grilled tomatoes and mushrooms.

Serves 4
450g/1lb potatoes

225g/8oz steamed or boiled cabbage or kale, shredded
1 egg, beaten
115g/4oz/1 cup Cheddar cheese, grated
freshly grated nutmeg
plain (all-purpose) flour, for coating
vegetable oil, for frying
salt and ground black pepper
lemon wedges, to serve

1 Put the potatoes in a large pan. Add water to cover and bring to the boil. Add salt, then reduce the heat to a simmer for about 15 minutes, or until the potatoes are tender, but do not let them get too soft. Drain and leave to cool.

2 Mix the mashed potato with the cabbage or kale, egg, cheese, nutmeg and seasoning. Shape into eight small burgers.

3 Chill for an hour or so, if possible, as this enables the rissoles to become firm and makes them easier to fry. Dredge them in the flour, shaking off the excess.

4 Heat a 1cm/½in layer of oil in a frying pan until it is really hot. Carefully slide the rissoles into the oil and fry in batches on each side for about 3 minutes until golden and crisp.

5 Remove the rissoles from the pan and drain on kitchen paper. Serve piping hot with wedges of freshly cut lemon.

Cook's Tip
You can flavour the rissoles with a stronger tasting cheese, if you prefer. Try using Stilton or Shropshire Blue in place of Cheddar.

Cabbage and Potato Charlotte

This cabbage and potato dish takes its name from the container with heart-shaped handles in which it is cooked. Any straight-sided dish, such as a soufflé dish, will do.

Serves 6
450g/1lb green or Savoy cabbage

30g/1oz/2 tbsp butter
1 medium onion, chopped
500g/1¼lb potatoes, peeled and quartered
1 large (US extra large) egg, beaten
15–30ml/1–2 tbsp milk, if needed
salt and ground black pepper

1 Preheat the oven to 190°C/375°F/ Gas 5. Lightly butter a 1.2 litre/2 pint/5 cup charlotte mould. Line the base with baking parchment and butter again.

2 Bring a pan of salted water to the boil. Remove 5–6 large leaves from the cabbage and add to the pan. Cook the leaves for 2 minutes until softened and bright green, then plunge them into cold water. Chop the remaining cabbage.

3 Melt the butter in a frying pan and cook the onion for 2–3 minutes until just soft. Stir in the chopped cabbage and cook, covered, over a medium heat for 10–15 minutes until tender.

4 Put the potatoes in a large pan of cold, salted water to cover and bring to the boil. Cook until the potatoes are tender, then drain. Mash with the egg and a little milk, if needed, until smooth, then stir in the cabbage mixture. Season to taste.

5 Dry the cabbage leaves and cut out the thickest part of the centre vein. Use the cabbage leaves to line the mould, saving one leaf for the top. Spoon the potato mixture into the dish, smoothing it evenly, then cover with the remaining cabbage leaf. Cover tightly with foil. Put the mould in a shallow roasting pan or a baking dish and pour in boiling water to come halfway up the side of the mould. Bake for 40 minutes.

6 To serve, remove the foil and place a serving plate over the mould. Holding the plate tightly against the mould, turn over together. Lift off the mould and peel off the paper.

Potato Rissoles Energy 423kcal/1762kJ; Protein 12.8g; Carbohydrate 30.7g, of which sugars 4.4g; Fat 27.9g, of which saturates 8.5g; Cholesterol 75mg; Calcium 272mg; Fibre 2.7g; Sodium 242mg.
Cabbage Charlotte Energy 131kcal/551kJ; Protein 3.7g; Carbohydrate 18g, of which sugars 5.3g; Fat 5.4g, of which saturates 3.1g; Cholesterol 43mg; Calcium 50mg; Fibre 2.6g; Sodium 64mg.

Mushroom Tart with Potato Pastry

Potato and cheese pastry combines well with a mushroom and broccoli filling to ensure this savoury flan is a favourite.

Serves 8
115g/4oz small broccoli florets
15ml/1 tbsp olive oil
3 shallots, finely chopped
175g/6oz mixed wild mushrooms, such as ceps, shiitake mushrooms and oyster mushrooms, sliced
2 eggs
200ml/7fl oz/scant 1 cup semi-skimmed (low-fat) milk
15ml/1 tbsp chopped fresh tarragon
50g/2oz/¼ cup grated Cheddar cheese
salt and ground black pepper
fresh herb sprigs, to garnish

For the pastry
75g/3oz/¾ cup brown rice flour
75g/3oz/¾ cup cornmeal
pinch of salt
75g/3oz/6 tbsp soft margarine
115g/4oz cold mashed potatoes
50g/2oz/½ cup grated Cheddar cheese

1 First make the pastry. Place the rice flour, cornmeal and salt in a mixing bowl and stir to mix. Lightly rub in the margarine with your fingertips until the mixture resembles breadcrumbs. Stir in the mashed potatoes and cheese and mix to form a smooth, soft dough. Wrap in a plastic bag and chill for 30 minutes.

2 Roll out the pastry between two sheets of baking parchment and use to line a 24cm/9½in loose-bottomed flan tin (pan), gently pressing the pastry into the sides of the tin. Carefully trim around the top edge of the pastry case with a sharp knife. Cover the pastry, and chill while making the filling.

3 Preheat the oven to 200°C/400°F/ Gas 6. Cook the broccoli florets in a pan of lightly salted, boiling water for 3 minutes. Drain and set aside. Heat the oil in a pan and cook the shallots for 3 minutes. Add the mushrooms and cook for 2 minutes.

4 Spoon into the pastry case (pie shell) and top with broccoli. Beat the eggs, milk, tarragon and seasoning together and pour over the vegetables. Top with cheese. Bake for 10 minutes, reduce the oven to 180°C/350°F/Gas 4 and bake for 30 minutes until lightly set. Serve warm or cold, garnished with fresh herbs.

Wild Mushroom Gratin with Beaufort Cheese, New Potatoes and Walnuts

This is one of the simplest and most delicious ways of cooking mushrooms. Serve this dish as the Swiss do, with new potatoes and gherkins.

Serves 4
900g/2lb small new or salad potatoes
50g/2oz/4 tbsp unsalted butter or 60ml/4 tbsp olive oil
350g/12oz/5 cups assorted wild and cultivated mushrooms, thinly sliced
175g/6oz Beaufort or Fontina cheese, thinly sliced
50g/2oz/½ cup broken walnuts, toasted
salt and ground black pepper
12 gherkins and mixed green salad leaves, to serve

1 Put the potatoes in a large pan. Add water to cover and bring to the boil. Add a little salt, then simmer for around 15 minutes, or until the potatoes are tender, but do not let them get too soft.

2 Drain the potatoes thoroughly and return them to the pan. Add a knob (pat) of butter or a splash of olive oil and cover to keep warm.

3 Heat the remaining butter or the olive oil in a large frying pan over a medium-high heat. Add the mushrooms and fry until their juices appear.

4 Increase the heat under the pan and cook the mushrooms briskly until most of their juices have cooked away. Season with salt and black pepper.

5 Meanwhile, preheat the grill (broiler). Arrange the cheese on top of the mushroom slices, place the pan under the grill and cook until bubbly and golden brown.

6 Sprinkle the gratin with the broken walnuts and serve immediately with the buttered potatoes and sliced gherkins. Serve a side dish of mixed green salad, if you like, to complete this meal.

Mushroom Tart Energy 253kcal/1051kJ; Protein 8.4g; Carbohydrate 19g, of which sugars 2.2g; Fat 15.6g, of which saturates 3.6g; Cholesterol 61mg; Calcium 145mg; Fibre 1.3g; Sodium 201mg.
Mushroom Gratin Energy 529kcal/2207kJ; Protein 18.4g; Carbohydrate 37g, of which sugars 3.5g; Fat 34.2g, of which saturates 17.3g; Cholesterol 71mg; Calcium 356mg; Fibre 3.7g; Sodium 440mg.

Herby Potatoes Baked with Tomatoes, Olives and Feta

This tasty potato dish comes from western Anatolia. Traditionally baked in an earthenware dish, it makes a fabulous accompaniment to vegetable kebabs. Or serve it on its own as a main course with a squeeze of lemon or a dollop of yogurt, and a green salad.

Serves 4–6

675g/1½lb organic new potatoes
15ml/1 tbsp butter
45ml/3 tbsp olive oil, plus extra
  for drizzling
3–4 garlic cloves, chopped

2 red onions, cut in half lengthways,
  in half again crossways, and
  sliced along the grain
5–10ml/1–2 tsp cumin
  seeds, crushed
5–10ml/1–2 tsp Turkish red
  pepper, or 1 fresh red chilli,
  seeded and chopped
10ml/2 tsp dried oregano
10ml/2 tsp sugar
15ml/1 tbsp white wine vinegar
400g/14oz can chopped
  tomatoes, drained of juice
12–16 black olives
115g/4oz feta cheese, crumbled
salt and ground black pepper
1 lemon, cut into wedges

1 Preheat the oven to 200°C/400°F/ Gas 6. Cook the potatoes for 15–20 minutes, until just tender. Drain and refresh in cold water. Peel and cut the potatoes into thick slices or bitesize wedges.

2 Heat the butter and 30ml/2 tbsp of the oil in a heavy pan, add the garlic and onions and cook until soft. Add the cumin seeds, red pepper or chilli and most of the oregano, then add the sugar, vinegar and tomatoes. Season generously with salt and pepper.

3 Put the sliced potatoes and olives into a baking dish and spoon over the tomato mixture. Crumble the feta cheese evenly over the top and sprinkle with the remaining oregano. Generously drizzle with the remaining olive oil, then bake in the preheated oven for 25–30 minutes.

4 Serve hot, straight from the oven, with lemon wedges to squeeze over.

Potatoes with Blue Cheese and Walnuts

Firm small potatoes, served in a creamy blue cheese sauce with the crunch of walnuts, make a great simple meal. For a change, serve it as a lunch dish or a light supper with a green salad.

Serves 4

450g/1lb small new or
  salad potatoes
1 small head of celery, sliced
1 small red onion, sliced
115g/4oz/1 cup blue
  cheese, mashed
150ml/¼ pint/⅔ cup single
  (light) cream
50g/2oz/½ cup walnut pieces
30ml/2 tbsp chopped
  fresh parsley
salt and ground black pepper

1 Cook the potatoes in their skins in a large pan with plenty of boiling water for about 15 minutes or until tender, adding the sliced celery and onion to the pan for the last 5 minutes or so of cooking.

2 Drain the vegetables well through a colander and put them into a shallow serving dish.

3 In a small pan, slowly melt the cheese in the cream, stirring occasionally. Do not allow the mixture to boil but heat it until it is simmering.

4 Check the sauce and season to taste with salt and ground black pepper. Pour it evenly over the vegetables in the dish and sprinkle over the walnut pieces and chopped fresh parsley. Serve hot, straight from the dish.

Cook's Tip
Use a combination of blue cheeses, such as Dolcelatte and Roquefort, or go for the distinctive flavour of Stilton on its own. If walnuts are not available, blue cheeses marry equally well with hazelnuts.

Herby Potatoes Energy 243kcal/1016kJ; Protein 6.3g; Carbohydrate 27.5g, of which sugars 9.3g; Fat 12.8g, of which saturates 5g; Cholesterol 19mg; Calcium 102mg; Fibre 2.9g; Sodium 447mg.
Potatoes with Walnuts Energy 350kcal/1459kJ; Protein 11.2g; Carbohydrate 21.9g, of which sugars 4.8g; Fat 24.8g, of which saturates 10.6g; Cholesterol 42mg; Calcium 236mg; Fibre 2.7g; Sodium 427mg.

Grilled Halloumi and Bean Salad with Skewered Potatoes

Halloumi, the hard, white salty goat's milk cheese that squeaks when you bite it, grills really well and is the perfect complement to fresh-tasting vegetables.

Serves 4
20 baby new potatoes, total
   weight about 300g/11oz
200g/7oz extra-fine green
   beans, trimmed
675g/1½lb broad (fava) beans,
   shelled weight 225g/8oz
200g/7oz halloumi cheese, cut
   into 5mm/¼in slices
1 garlic clove, crushed to a paste
   with a large pinch of salt
90ml/6 tbsp olive oil
5ml/1 tsp cider vinegar or white
   wine vinegar
15g/½oz/½ cup fresh basil
   leaves, shredded
45ml/3 tbsp chopped fresh savory
2 spring onions (scallions),
   finely sliced
salt and ground black pepper

1 Thread five potatoes on to each skewer, and cook in a large pan of salted boiling water for about 7 minutes or until almost tender. Add the green beans and cook for 3 minutes more. Add the broad beans and cook for just 2 minutes. Drain all the vegetables in a large colander.

2 Refresh the cooked broad beans under cold water. Pop each broad bean out of its skin to reveal the bright green inner bean. Place in a bowl, cover and set aside.

3 Preheat a grill (broiler) or griddle. Place the halloumi slices and the potato skewers in a wide dish. Whisk the garlic and oil together with a generous grinding of black pepper. Add to the dish and toss the halloumi and potato skewers until thoroughly coated in the mixture.

4 Cook the cheese and potato skewers under the grill or on the griddle for about 2 minutes on each side.

5 Add the vinegar to the oil and garlic remaining in the dish and whisk to mix. Toss in the beans, herbs and spring onions, with the cooked halloumi. Serve with the potato skewers.

Potato Gnocchi with Simple Tomato and Butter Sauce

Potato gnocchi make a substantial and tasty alternative to pasta. In this dish they are served with a very simple, but delicious, fresh tomato sauce.

Serves 4
675g/1½lb floury potatoes
2 egg yolks
75g/3oz/¾ cup plain
   (all-purpose) flour
60ml/4 tbsp finely chopped fresh
   parsley, to garnish

For the sauce
25g/1oz/2 tbsp butter, melted
450g/1lb plum tomatoes, peeled,
   seeded and chopped
salt

1 Preheat the oven to 200°C/400°F/ Gas 6. Scrub the potatoes, then bake them in their skins in the oven for 1 hour or until the flesh feels soft when pricked with a fork.

2 While the potatoes are still warm, cut them in half and gently squeeze the flesh into a bowl, or use a spoon to scrape the flesh out of the shells. Mash the potato well, then season with a little salt. Add the egg yolks and mix lightly with a fork or spoon.

3 Add the flour and mix to a rough dough. Place on a floured work surface and knead for around 5 minutes until the dough is smooth and elastic. Shape the dough into small thumb-sized shapes by making long rolls and cutting them into evenly sized segments. Press each of these with the back of a fork to give a ridged effect. Place the gnocchi on a floured work surface.

4 Preheat the oven to 140°C/275°F/Gas 1. Cook the gnocchi in small batches in barely simmering, slightly salted water for about 10 minutes. Remove with a slotted spoon, drain well and transfer to a dish. Cover and keep hot in the oven.

5 To make the sauce, heat the butter in a small pan for 1 minute, then add the tomatoes and cook over a low heat until the juice starts to run. Sprinkle the gnocchi with chopped parsley and serve with the sauce.

Halloumi and Bean Energy 393kcal/1635kJ; Protein 16.5g; Carbohydrate 20.8g, of which sugars 3.4g; Fat 27.7g, of which saturates 9.4g; Cholesterol 29mg; Calcium 263mg; Fibre 6.3g; Sodium 215mg.
Gnocchi with Sauce Energy 278kcal/1174kJ; Protein 6.9g; Carbohydrate 45.3g, of which sugars 6g; Fat 9g, of which saturates 4.4g; Cholesterol 114mg; Calcium 57mg; Fibre 3.4g; Sodium 72mg.

Potato Gnocchi

Gnocchi are little Italian dumplings made either with mashed potato and flour, or with semolina. To ensure that they are light and fluffy, take care not to overmix the dough.

Serves 4–6
1kg/2¼lb waxy potatoes

250–300g/9–11oz/2¼–2¾ cups
  plain (all-purpose) flour, plus
  more if necessary
1 egg
pinch of freshly grated nutmeg
25g/1oz/2 tbsp butter
salt
fresh basil leaves, to garnish
Parmesan cheese cut in shavings,
  to garnish

1 Cook the potatoes in their skins in a large pan of boiling, salted water until tender but not falling apart. Drain and peel while the potatoes are still hot.

2 Spread a layer of flour on a work surface. Pass the hot potatoes through a food mill, dropping them directly on to the flour. Sprinkle with about half of the remaining flour and mix in very lightly. Break the egg into the mixture.

3 Finally, add the nutmeg to the dough and knead lightly, adding more flour if the mixture is too loose. When the dough is light to the touch and no longer moist it is ready to be rolled. Divide the dough into four pieces. On a lightly floured surface, form each into a roll about 2cm/¾in in diameter. Cut the rolls crossways into even pieces of about 2cm/¾in in length.

4 Hold an ordinary table fork with tines sideways, leaning on the board. Then one by one, press and roll the gnocchi lightly along the tines of the fork towards the points, making ridges on one side, and a depression from your thumb on the other.

5 Bring a large pan of salted water to the boil, then drop in about half the gnocchi. When they rise to the surface, after 3–4 minutes, they are done. Lift them out with a slotted spoon, drain well, and place in a warmed serving bowl. Dot with butter. Cover to keep warm while cooking the remainder. As soon as they are cooked, toss the gnocchi with the butter, garnish with Parmesan and basil leaves, and serve immediately.

Potato Gnocchi with Gorgonzola

Potato gnocchi are prepared all over Italy with different ingredients used in different regions. These are delicious with a creamy cheese sauce.

Serves 4
450g/1lb potatoes, unpeeled
1 large (US extra large) egg
115g/4oz/1 cup plain
  (all-purpose) flour

fresh thyme sprigs, to garnish
salt and ground black pepper

For the sauce
115g/4oz Gorgonzola cheese
60ml/4 tbsp double
  (heavy) cream
15ml/1 tbsp fresh
  thyme, chopped
60 ml/4 tbsp freshly grated
  Parmesan cheese, to serve

1 Cook the potatoes in boiling, salted water for 20 minutes until they are tender. Drain and, when cool, remove the skins.

2 Force the potatoes through a sieve (strainer) into a mixing bowl. Season and then beat in the egg until combined. Add the flour a little at a time, stirring well with a wooden spoon after each addition until you have a smooth dough.

3 Turn the dough out on to a floured surface and knead for about 3 minutes, adding more flour if necessary, until it is smooth and soft and not sticky to the touch.

4 Divide the dough into six equal pieces. Flour your hands and gently roll each piece into a log shape measuring 15–20cm/ 6–8in long and 2.5cm/1in around. Cut each log into six to eight pieces, about 2.5cm/1in long, then gently roll each piece in the flour. Form into gnocchi by gently pressing on to the floured surface with the tines of a fork to leave clear ridges in the dough.

5 To cook, drop the gnocchi into a pan of boiling water about 12 at a time. Once they rise to the surface, after about 2 minutes, cook for 4–5 minutes more. Remove and drain.

6 Place the Gorgonzola, cream and thyme in a large frying pan and heat gently until the cheese melts to form a thick, creamy consistency. Add the drained gnocchi and toss well to combine. Serve with Parmesan and garnish with thyme.

Potato Gnocchi Energy 296kcal/1254kJ; Protein 7.8g; Carbohydrate 59.2g, of which sugars 2.8g; Fat 4.7g, of which saturates 2.3g; Cholesterol 39mg; Calcium 74mg; Fibre 3g; Sodium 52mg.
Gorgonzola Gnocchi Energy 430kcal/1801kJ; Protein 18.1g; Carbohydrate 40.9g, of which sugars 2.3g; Fat 23.6g, of which saturates 13.5g; Cholesterol 104mg; Calcium 386mg; Fibre 2g; Sodium 562mg.

Spiced Pumpkin and Potato Gnocchi

Pumpkin adds a sweetness to these potato gnocchi, which are superb on their own or served with a side salad.

Serves 4

450g/1lb pumpkin, peeled, seeded and chopped
450g/1lb potatoes, boiled
2 egg yolks
200g/7oz/1¾ cups plain (all-purpose) flour, plus more if necessary
pinch of ground allspice
1.5ml/¼ tsp cinnamon
pinch of freshly grated nutmeg
finely grated rind of ½ orange
salt and ground pepper

For the sauce

30ml/2 tbsp olive oil
1 shallot, finely chopped
175g/6oz/2½ cups fresh chanterelles, sliced, or 15g/½oz/½ cup dried, soaked in warm water for 20 minutes, then drained
10ml/2 tsp almond butter
150ml/¼ pint/⅔ cup crème fraîche
75ml/5 tbsp chopped fresh parsley
50g/2oz/½ cup Parmesan cheese, freshly grated

1 Wrap the pumpkin in foil and bake at 180°C/350°F/Gas 4 for 30 minutes. Pass the pumpkin and cooked potatoes through a food mill into a bowl. Add the egg yolks, flour, spices, orange rind and seasoning and mix well to make a soft dough. If the mixture is too loose, add a little flour to stiffen it.

2 To make the sauce, heat the oil in a pan and fry the shallot until soft. Add the chanterelles and cook briefly, then add the almond butter. Stir to melt and stir in the crème fraîche. Simmer briefly, add the parsley and season to taste. Keep hot.

3 Flour a work surface. Spoon the gnocchi dough into a piping (pastry) bag fitted with a 1cm/½in plain nozzle. Pipe on to the flour to make a 15cm/6in sausage. Roll in flour and cut crossways into 2.5cm/1in pieces. Repeat. Mark each piece lightly with a fork and drop into a pan of fast boiling, salted water.

4 The gnocchi are done when they rise to the surface, after 3–4 minutes. Drain and turn into bowls. Spoon the sauce over, sprinkle with Parmesan, and serve immediately.

Orecchiette with Potatoes and Rocket

This hearty potato dish is from the south-east of Italy. Serve it as a main course with country bread. Some delicatessens and supermarkets sell a farmhouse-style Italian loaf called pugliese, which would be most appropriate.

Serves 4–6

45ml/3 tbsp olive oil
1 small onion, finely chopped
300g/11oz canned chopped Italian plum tomatoes or passata (bottled strained tomatoes)
2.5ml/½ tsp dried oregano
pinch of chilli powder or cayenne pepper
about 30ml/2 tbsp red or white wine (optional)
2 potatoes, total weight about 200g/7oz, diced
300g/11oz/2¾ cups dried orecchiette
2 garlic cloves, finely chopped
150g/5oz rocket (arugula) leaves, stalks removed, shredded
90g/3½oz/scant ½ cup ricotta cheese
salt and ground black pepper
freshly grated Pecorino cheese, to serve

1 Heat 15ml/1 tbsp of the olive oil in a medium pan, add half the finely chopped onion and cook gently, stirring frequently, for about 5 minutes until softened. Add the canned tomatoes or passata, oregano and chilli powder or cayenne pepper to the onion. Pour the wine over, if using, and add a little salt and pepper to taste. Cover and simmer for about 15 minutes.

2 Bring a large pan of salted water to the boil. Add the potatoes and pasta. Stir well and let the water return to the boil. Lower the heat and simmer for 15 minutes, or according to the packet instructions, until the pasta is cooked.

3 Heat the remaining oil in a large frying pan, add the rest of the onion and the garlic and fry for 2–3 minutes, stirring occasionally. Add the rocket, toss over the heat for about 2 minutes until wilted, then stir in the tomato sauce and the ricotta. Mix well.

4 Drain the pasta and potatoes, add both to the pan of sauce and toss to mix. Taste for seasoning and serve immediately in warmed bowls, with grated Pecorino handed separately.

Pumpkin Gnocchi Energy 553kcal/2317kJ; Protein 15.6g; Carbohydrate 61.7g, of which sugars 5.9g; Fat 28.8g, of which saturates 14.7g; Cholesterol 156mg; Calcium 299mg; Fibre 4.5g; Sodium 166mg.
Orecchiette Energy 584kcal/2451kJ; Protein 18.9g; Carbohydrate 65.4g, of which sugars 3.5g; Fat 29.2g, of which saturates 7.1g; Cholesterol 19mg; Calcium 311mg; Fibre 3.3g; Sodium 260mg.

Pasta with Pesto and Potatoes

This is one of the traditional ways to serve pesto in Liguria. Although the mix of pasta and potatoes may seem odd, it is delicious with the rich pesto sauce.

Serves 4
50g/2oz/½ cup pine nuts
2 large garlic cloves, chopped
90g/3½oz fresh basil leaves
90ml/6 tbsp extra virgin olive oil
50g/2oz/⅔ cup Parmesan cheese
40g/1½oz/½ cup freshly grated
   Pecorino cheese

For the pasta mixture
275g/10oz waxy potatoes, thickly
   sliced or cut into
   1cm/½in cubes
200g/7oz fine green beans
350g/12oz dried trenette,
   linguine, tagliatelle
   or tagliarini
salt and ground black pepper

To serve
extra virgin olive oil
pine nuts, toasted
Parmesan Cheese
basil leaves, to garnish

1 Toast the pine nuts in a dry frying pan until golden. Place in a mortar with the garlic and a pinch of salt, and crush with a pestle. Add the basil and add a little oil as you work the mixture to a paste. Add the Parmesan and Pecorino and the remaining oil.

2 Bring a pan of lightly salted water to the boil and add the potatoes. Cook for 10–12 minutes, until tender. Add the green beans to the pan for the last 5–6 minutes of cooking.

3 Meanwhile, cook the pasta in boiling salted water for 8–12 minutes, or according to the packet instructions, until just tender. Times vary according to the pasta shapes.

4 Drain the pasta, potatoes and beans. Place in a large bowl and toss with two-thirds of the pesto. Season with pepper and sprinkle basil leaves over the top. Serve with the rest of the pesto, extra olive oil, pine nuts and grated Parmesan.

> **Cook's Tip**
> To freeze pesto, make it without the cheeses, then freeze.
> To use, simply thaw, then stir in the cheeses.

Roasted Red Pepper Tortilla

This comforting and delicious recipe relies on only a few basic ingredients, but the mixture of eggs, potatoes and silky red peppers is always a winner. This is perfect when served with a seasonal salad for a tasty and sophisticated lunchtime treat.

Serves 2
450g/1lb potatoes, peeled and
   cut into small chunks
50ml/2fl oz/¼ cup olive oil
1 large onion, finely sliced
2 red (bell) peppers, halved
   and seeded
4 eggs
salt and ground black pepper

1 Season the potatoes well with salt and pepper. Heat half the oil in a non-stick frying pan and cook the potatoes over a medium heat for 15 minutes until starting to brown. Make sure to keep the potatoes moving so that they do not stick to the bottom of the pan.

2 Meanwhile, in another pan, heat half the remaining oil and fry the onion slices for about 20 minutes until really soft.

3 Grill (broil) the peppers for 10 minutes until charred on the outside. Put in a plastic bag, seal, and leave for around 10 minutes to steam.

4 Beat the eggs in a bowl, add the potatoes and onions and stir well. Season to taste.

5 Peel the skins off the peppers, roughly chop the flesh and add to the egg, potato and onion mixture.

6 Heat the remaining oil in the non-stick frying pan and pour in the egg and potato mixture. Cook over a low heat for around 10 minutes, until beginning to set.

7 Invert a large plate or lid over the pan and carefully turn the omelette over on to it . Slide the omelette back into the pan and cook on the other side for a further 3–4 minutes until set.

8 Serve hot from the pan, cut into wedges and accompanied by a light, seasonal salad.

Pasta with Pesto Energy 658kcal/2760kJ; Protein 20g; Carbohydrate 78.6g, of which sugars 5.9g; Fat 31.5g, of which saturates 5.8g; Cholesterol 13mg; Calcium 240mg; Fibre 5.7g; Sodium 154mg.
Pepper Tortilla Energy 515kcal/2130kJ; Protein 22.6g; Carbohydrate 38.6g, of which sugars 5.6g; Fat 40.7g, of which saturates 14.2g; Cholesterol 47.3mg; Calcium 281mg; Fibre 3.5g; Sodium 68mg.

Potato and Onion Tortilla

This deep-set omelette with sliced potatoes and onions is the best-known Spanish tortilla and makes a deliciously simple meal when served with a leafy salad and crusty bread. Use waxy potatoes rather than the floury variety as they will hold their shape better when cooked.

Serves 6

800g/1¾lb medium potatoes
100ml/3½fl oz/scant ½ cup
    extra virgin olive oil
2 onions, thinly sliced
salt and ground black pepper
6 eggs

1 Thinly slice the potatoes. Heat 75ml/5 tbsp of the oil in a frying pan and cook the potatoes, turning frequently, for about 10 minutes.

2 Add the onions to the pan, and continue to cook gently for a further 10 minutes, until the vegetables are tender. Season with salt and ground black pepper.

3 Meanwhile, beat the eggs in a large bowl with a little salt and black pepper. Transfer the potatoes and onions into the eggs and mix gently. Leave to stand for 10 minutes.

4 Wipe out the pan with kitchen paper and heat the remaining oil in it. Pour the egg mixture into the pan and spread it out in an even layer.

5 Cover the pan and cook over a very gentle heat for about 20 minutes, until the eggs are just set. Serve immediately, cut into wedges, or leave to cool completely before serving.

Variation
Tortilla are often made with a variety of other ingredients – chopped red or yellow (bell) peppers, cooked peas, pitted olives, corn, or grated Cheddar or Gruyère cheese can all be added to the mixture in step 3, if you like.

Potato Tortilla

The classic tortilla can be found in every tapas bar in Spain. The inclusion of potatoes makes it dense and very satisfying. It can be eaten in wedges with a fork – a meal in itself with salad – or cut up into chunks and speared, to be enjoyed as a snack with drinks.

Serves 6

450g/1lb small waxy
    potatoes, peeled
1 Spanish (Bermuda) onion
45ml/3 tbsp vegetable oil
4 large eggs
salt and ground black pepper
fresh flat leaf parsley or tomato
    wedges, to garnish

1 Using a sharp knife, cut the potatoes into thin slices and slice the onion into thin rings. Heat 30ml/2 tbsp of the oil in a 20cm/8in heavy frying pan.

2 Add the potatoes and the onions to the pan and cook over a low heat for 20 minutes, or until the potato slices are just tender. Stir from time to time to prevent the potatoes sticking. Remove from the heat.

3 In a large bowl, beat together the eggs with a little salt and pepper. When the cooked potatoes and onion have cooled a little, stir them into the eggs.

4 Clean the frying pan with kitchen paper then heat the remaining oil and pour in the potato mixture. Cook very gently for 5–8 minutes until set underneath. During cooking, lift the edges of the tortilla with a spatula, and allow any uncooked egg to run underneath. Shake the pan from side to side, to prevent sticking.

5 Place a large heatproof plate upside down over the pan, invert the tortilla on to the plate and then slide it back into the pan. Cook for 2–3 minutes more, until the underside of the tortilla is golden brown.

6 Cut the tortilla into wedges and serve immediately or leave until warm or cold. Serve garnished with fresh flat leaf parsley or tomato wedges.

Potato and Onion Tortilla Energy 443kcal/1848kJ; Protein 16g; Carbohydrate 32.4g, of which sugars 3.6g; Fat 28.1g, of which saturates 12.3g; Cholesterol 49mg; Calcium 226mg; Fibre 1.9g; Sodium 728mg.
Potato Tortilla Energy 163kcal/681kJ; Protein 5.8g; Carbohydrate 14.7g, of which sugars 2.9g; Fat 9.5g, of which saturates 1.9g; Cholesterol 127mg; Calcium 32mg; Fibre 1.2g; Sodium 56mg.

Potato and Onion Tortilla with Broad Beans

Adding chopped herbs and a few skinned broad beans to the classic potato tortilla makes this a very summery dish to enjoy at lunch, or cut it into small pieces and serve as an appetizer.

Serves 2
45ml/3 tbsp olive oil
2 Spanish (Bermuda) onions,
    thinly sliced
300g/11oz waxy potatoes, cut
    into 1cm/½in dice
250g/9oz/1¾ cups shelled
    broad (fava) beans
5ml/1 tsp chopped fresh thyme or
    summer savory
6 large eggs
45ml/3 tbsp mixed chopped
    chives and chopped flat
    leaf parsley
salt and ground black pepper

1 Heat 30ml/2 tbsp of the oil in a 23cm/9in deep non-stick frying pan. Add the onions and potatoes and stir to coat. Cover and cook gently, stirring frequently, for 20–25 minutes until the potatoes are tender. Do not let the mixture brown.

2 Meanwhile, cook the beans in boiling salted water for 5 minutes. Drain well and set aside to cool.

3 When the beans are cool enough to handle, peel off the grey outer skins. Add the beans to the frying pan, together with the thyme or summer savory, and season with salt and pepper to taste. Stir well to mix and cook for a further 2–3 minutes.

4 Beat the eggs with salt and pepper to taste and the mixed herbs, then pour over the potatoes and onions and increase the heat slightly. Cook gently until the egg on the bottom sets and browns, gently pulling the omelette away from the sides of the pan and tilting it to allow the uncooked egg to run underneath.

5 Invert the tortilla on to a plate. Add the remaining oil to the pan and heat until hot. Slip the tortilla back into the pan, uncooked side down, and cook for another 3–5 minutes to allow the underneath to brown. Slide the tortilla out on to a plate. Divide as wished, and serve warm rather than piping hot.

Chilli Cheese and Potato Tortilla with Fresh Tomato Salsa

Good warm or cold, this is like a sliced potato quiche without the pastry base, spiked with chilli. The salsa can be made without the chilli, if you prefer. Use a firm but not hard cheese, such as Double Gloucester, Monterey Jack or Manchego.

Serves 4
45ml/3 tbsp sunflower or
    olive oil
1 small onion, thinly sliced
2–3 fresh green jalapeño chillies,
    seeded and sliced
200g/7oz cold cooked potato,
    thinly sliced
120g/4¼oz/generous 1 cup
    cheese, grated
6 eggs, beaten
salt and ground black pepper
fresh herbs, to garnish

For the salsa
500g/1¼lb fresh flavoursome
    tomatoes, peeled, seeded and
    finely chopped
1 fresh mild green chilli, seeded
    and finely chopped
2 garlic cloves, crushed
45ml/3 tbsp chopped fresh
    coriander (cilantro)
juice of 1 lime
2.5ml/½ tsp salt

1 To make the salsa, put the tomatoes in a bowl and add the chopped chilli, garlic, coriander, lime juice and salt. Mix well and set aside.

2 Heat 15ml/1 tbsp of the oil in a large omelette pan and gently fry the onion and jalapeños for 5 minutes, stirring until softened. Add the potato and cook for another 5 minutes until lightly browned, keeping the slices whole.

3 Using a slotted spoon, transfer the vegetables to a warm plate. Wipe the pan with kitchen paper, then add the remaining oil and heat until really hot. Return the vegetables to the pan. Sprinkle the cheese over the top. Season.

4 Pour in the beaten eggs, making sure that they seep under the vegetables. Cook the tortilla over a low heat, without stirring, until set. Serve hot or cold, cut into wedges, garnished with fresh herbs and with the salsa on the side.

Potato Tortilla Energy 673kcal/2812kJ; Protein 34.9g; Carbohydrate 59.2g, of which sugars 18.1g; Fat 35.2g, of which saturates 7.3g; Cholesterol 571mg; Calcium 272mg; Fibre 14.3g; Sodium 252mg.
Cheese Tortilla Energy 375kcal/1563kJ; Protein 19.3g; Carbohydrate 13.5g, of which sugars 5.7g; Fat 27.1g, of which saturates 10g; Cholesterol 315mg; Calcium 305mg; Fibre 2.6g; Sodium 589mg.

Potato, Red Onion and Feta Frittata

This Italian omelette is cooked with vegetables and crumbly feta cheese, and is given real substance by the addition of golden new potatoes. Cut it into generous wedges and serve with crusty bread and a tasty tomato salad.

Serves 2–4
25ml/1½ tbsp olive oil
1 red onion, sliced
350g/12oz cooked new potatoes, halved or quartered, if large
6 eggs, lightly beaten
115g/4oz/1 cup feta cheese, diced
salt and ground black pepper

1 Heat the oil in a large heavy, flameproof frying pan. Add the onion and cook for 5 minutes until softened, stirring occasionally.

2 Add the potatoes and cook for a further 5 minutes until golden, stirring to prevent them sticking. Spread the mixture evenly over the base of the pan.

3 Preheat the grill (broiler) to high. Season the beaten eggs, then pour them over the onion and potatoes. Sprinkle the cheese on top and cook over a moderate heat for 5–6 minutes until the eggs are set and the base of the frittata is lightly golden.

4 Place the pan under the preheated grill (protect the pan handle with a double layer of foil if it is not flameproof) and cook the top of the omelette for about 3 minutes until it is set and golden. Serve the frittata warm or cold, cut into wedges.

> **Cook's Tip**
> *Eggs are an important source of vitamin B12, which is vital for the nervous system and the development of red blood cells. They also supply other B vitamins, zinc and selenium and a useful amount of iron. It is beneficial to eat a food rich in vitamin C at the same time in order to help the absorption of iron. Do not eat too many eggs, though — try not to exceed a maximum of three per week.*

Indian Spiced Potato, Corn and Pea Omelette

This delicately spiced Indian potato omelette is a delicious and intriguing twist on the traditional Spanish tortilla. The distinctive warming aroma of cumin and the bulk given by the corn, potatoes and peas make this a truly memorable dish.

Serves 4–6
30ml/2 tbsp vegetable oil
1 onion, finely chopped
2.5ml/½ tsp ground cumin
1 garlic clove, crushed

1 or 2 fresh green chillies, finely chopped
a few coriander (cilantro) sprigs, chopped, plus extra, to garnish
1 firm tomato, chopped
1 small potato, cubed and boiled
25g/1oz/¼ cup cooked peas
25g/1oz/¼ cup cooked corn, or drained canned corn
2 eggs, beaten
25g/1oz/¼ cup grated Cheddar cheese or Monterey Jack
salt and ground black pepper

1 Heat the oil in a wok or omelette pan, add the onion, cumin, garlic, chillies, coriander, tomato, potato, peas and corn. Mix well.

2 Cook over a medium heat, stirring, for 5 minutes, until the potato and tomato are almost tender. Season well with salt and ground black pepper.

3 Preheat the grill (broiler) to high. Increase the heat under the pan and pour in the beaten eggs. Reduce the heat to medium, cover and cook until the bottom layer is brown. Turn the omelette over, then sprinkle with the grated cheese. Place under the hot grill and cook until the egg sets and the cheese has melted.

4 Garnish the omelette with sprigs of coriander and serve with salad for a light lunch, or on its own as a wholesome breakfast.

> **Variation**
> *You can use any vegetable with the potatoes. Try thickly sliced button (white) mushrooms, which can be added in step 1.*

Potato and Feta Frittata Energy 289kcal/1207kJ; Protein 15.5g; Carbohydrate 15.7g, of which sugars 2.4g; Fat 18.9g, of which saturates 7g; Cholesterol 306mg; Calcium 155mg; Fibre 1.1g; Sodium 529mg.
Spicy Omelette Energy 93kcal/388kJ; Protein 4g; Carbohydrate 3.7g, of which sugars 1.2g; Fat 7.1g, of which saturates 1.9g; Cholesterol 67mg; Calcium 46mg; Fibre 0.6g; Sodium 104mg.

Potato and Cauliflower Curry

This is a hot and spicy vegetable curry, loaded with potatoes, cauliflower and broad beans, and is especially tasty when served with cooked rice, a few poppadums and a cooling cucumber raita.

Serves 4

1 onion, sliced
1 large potato, chopped
15ml/1 tbsp curry powder,
  mild or hot
1 cauliflower, cut into
  small florets
600ml/1 pint/2½ cups
  vegetable stock
275g/10oz can broad
  (fava) beans
juice of ½ lemon (optional)
salt and ground black pepper
fresh coriander (cilantro) sprig,
  to garnish
plain rice, to serve

2 garlic cloves, chopped
2.5cm/1in piece fresh root ginger
1 fresh green chilli, seeded
  and chopped
30ml/2 tbsp oil

1 Blend the chopped garlic, ginger, chopped chilli with 15ml/1 tbsp of the oil in a food processor or blender until the mixture forms a smooth paste.

2 In a large, heavy pan, fry the sliced onion and chopped potato in the remaining oil for 5 minutes, until the onion is soft and the potato is starting to brown, then stir in the spice paste and curry powder. Cook for another minute.

3 Add the cauliflower florets to the onion and potato and stir well until they are thoroughly combined with the spicy mixture, then pour in the stock and bring to the boil over medium to high heat.

4 Season well, cover and simmer for 10 minutes. Add the beans with the liquid from the can and cook, uncovered, for a further 10 minutes.

5 Check the seasoning and adjust if necessary. Add a good squeeze of lemon juice and give the curry a final stir.

6 Serve immediately, on preheated plates, garnished with fresh coriander sprigs and accompanied by plain boiled rice.

Potato Curry with Yogurt

Variations of this simple Indian potato curry are popular in Singapore, where fusion dishes like this one cater for a community that includes people from all over Asia, as well as from Europe and the Americas.

Serves 4

6 garlic cloves, chopped
25g/1oz fresh root ginger, peeled
  and chopped
30ml/2 tbsp ghee, or 15ml/1 tbsp
  oil and 15g/½oz/1 tbsp butter
6 shallots, halved lengthways and
  sliced along the grain
2 fresh green chillies, seeded
  and finely sliced

10ml/2 tsp sugar
a handful of fresh or dried
  curry leaves
2 cinnamon sticks
5–10ml/1–2 tsp
  ground turmeric
15ml/1 tbsp garam masala
500g/1¼lb waxy potatoes, cut
  into bitesize pieces
2 tomatoes, peeled, seeded
  and quartered
250ml/8fl oz/1 cup Greek
  (US strained plain) yogurt
salt and ground black pepper
5ml/1 tsp red chilli powder, and
  fresh coriander (cilantro) and
  mint leaves, finely chopped,
  to garnish
1 lemon, quartered, to serve

1 Using a mortar and pestle or a food processor, grind the garlic and ginger to a coarse paste. Heat the ghee in a heavy pan and stir in the shallots and chillies, until soft and fragrant.

2 Add the garlic and ginger paste with the sugar, and stir until the mixture begins to colour. Stir in the curry leaves, cinnamon sticks, turmeric and garam masala, and toss in the cubed potatoes, making sure that they are thoroughly coated in the ground spice mixture.

3 Pour in just enough cold water to cover the potatoes. Bring to the boil, then reduce the heat and simmer until the potatoes are just cooked – they should still have a bite to them.

4 Season with salt and ground black pepper to taste. Gently toss in the tomatoes to heat them through. Fold in the yogurt so that it is streaky. Sprinkle with the chilli powder, coriander and mint. Serve immediately from the pan, with lemon to squeeze over.

Potato Curry Energy 231kcal/967kJ; Protein 6.7g; Carbohydrate 26.2g, of which sugars 7.4g; Fat 12.4g, of which saturates 4.1g; Cholesterol 0mg; Calcium 110mg; Fibre 2g; Sodium 63mg.
Broad Bean Curry Energy 194kcal/813kJ; Protein 11.5g; Carbohydrate 20.9g, of which sugars 4.8g; Fat 7.7g, of which saturates 1g; Cholesterol 0mg; Calcium 96mg; Fibre 8.1g; Sodium 40mg.

Black-eyed Bean and Potato Curry

Nutty-flavoured black-eyed beans make a nutritious supper dish, especially when mixed with potatoes. This hot and spicy combination will be ideal for an autumn or winter evening.

Serves 4–6
2 potatoes
225g/8oz/1¼ cups black-eyed beans (peas), soaked overnight and drained
1.5ml/¼ tsp bicarbonate of soda (baking soda)
5ml/1 tsp five-spice powder
1.5ml/¼ tsp asafoetida
2 onions, finely chopped
2.5cm/1in piece fresh root ginger, crushed
a few fresh mint leaves
450ml/¾ pint/scant 2 cups water
60ml/4 tbsp vegetable oil
2.5ml/½ tsp each ground cumin, ground coriander, ground turmeric and chilli powder
4 fresh green chillies, chopped
75ml/5 tbsp tamarind juice
115g/4oz/4 cups fresh coriander (cilantro), chopped
2 firm tomatoes, chopped
salt

1 Cut the potatoes into cubes and boil in lightly salted water until tender.

2 Place the drained black-eyed beans in a heavy pan and add the bicarbonate of soda, five-spice powder and asafoetida. Add the chopped onions, crushed root ginger, mint leaves and the measured water. Simmer until the beans are soft. Remove any excess water and reserve.

3 Heat the oil in a frying pan. Gently fry the ground cumin and coriander, the turmeric and chilli powder with the green chillies and tamarind juice, until they are well blended and releasing their fragrances.

4 Pour the spice mixture over the black-eyed beans and mix well.

5 Add the potatoes, fresh coriander, tomatoes and salt. Mix well, and, if necessary, thin with a little reserved water. Reheat and serve.

Vegetable and Coconut Milk Curry

Fragrant jasmine rice is the perfect accompaniment for this spicy and flavoursome vegetable curry.

Serves 4
10ml/2 tsp vegetable oil
400ml/14fl oz/1⅔ cups coconut milk
300ml/½ pint/1¼ cups vegetable stock
225g/8oz new potatoes, halved
8 baby corn cobs
5ml/1 tsp sugar
185g/6½oz/1¼ cups broccoli florets
1 red (bell) pepper, seeded and sliced lengthways
115g/4oz spinach, tough stalks removed, leaves shredded
30ml/2 tbsp chopped fresh coriander (cilantro)

salt and ground black pepper
cooked fragrant jasmine rice, to serve

For the spice paste
1 fresh red chilli, seeded and chopped
3 fresh green chillies, seeded and chopped
1 lemon grass stalk, outer leaves removed and lower 5cm/2in finely chopped
2 shallots, chopped
finely grated rind of 1 lime
2 garlic cloves, chopped
5ml/1 tsp ground coriander
2.5ml/½ tsp ground cumin
1cm/½in piece fresh galangal, finely chopped, or 2.5ml/½ tsp dried galangal (optional)
30ml/2 tbsp chopped fresh coriander (cilantro)

1 Make the spice paste. Place all the ingredients in a food processor and process until you have a coarse paste. Heat the oil in a large, heavy pan. Add the spice paste and stir-fry for 1–2 minutes. Pour in the coconut milk and vegetable stock. Boil, then add the potatoes and simmer gently for about 15 minutes, until almost tender.

2 Add the baby corn cobs to the potatoes, season with salt and pepper to taste, then cook for 2 minutes. Stir in the sugar, broccoli and red pepper, and cook for 2 minutes more, until the vegetables are tender.

3 Stir in the shredded spinach and half the fresh coriander. Cook for 2 minutes, then spoon into a serving dish and garnish with the remaining fresh coriander. Serve immediately with the jasmine rice.

Black-eyed Bean Curry Energy 266kcal/1118kJ; Protein 11.8g; Carbohydrate 36.8g, of which sugars 8.5g; Fat 9g, of which saturates 1.1g; Cholesterol 0mg; Calcium 110mg; Fibre 8.8g; Sodium 28mg.
Vegetable Curry Energy 198kcal/827kJ; Protein 3.4g; Carbohydrate 19.2g, of which sugars 18.7g; Fat 12.6g, of which saturates 1.8g; Cholesterol 0mg; Calcium 191mg; Fibre 6.4g; Sodium 312mg.

Vegetable Korma

Here the aim is to produce a subtle, aromatic curry rather than an assault on the senses.

Serves 4

50g/2oz/¼ cup butter
2 onions, sliced
2 garlic cloves, crushed
2.5cm/1in piece fresh root
  ginger, grated
5ml/1 tsp ground cumin
15ml/1 tbsp ground coriander
6 cardamom pods
5cm/2in piece of cinnamon stick
5ml/1 tsp ground turmeric
1 fresh red chilli, seeded and
  finely chopped

1 potato, peeled and cut into
  2.5cm/1in cubes
1 small aubergine
  (eggplant), chopped
115g/4oz/1½ cups mushrooms,
  thickly sliced
175ml/6fl oz/¾ cup water
115g/4oz green beans, cut into
  2.5cm/1in lengths
60ml/4 tbsp natural (plain) yogurt
150ml/¼ pint/⅔ cup double
  (heavy) cream
5ml/1 tsp garam masala
salt and ground black pepper
fresh coriander (cilantro) sprigs,
  to garnish
boiled rice and poppadums,
  to serve

1 Melt the butter in a heavy pan. Add the onions and cook for 5 minutes until soft.

2 Add the garlic and ginger and cook for 2 minutes, then stir in the cumin, coriander, cardamom pods, cinnamon stick, turmeric and finely chopped chilli. Cook, stirring, for 1–2 minutes.

3 Add the potato cubes, aubergine and mushrooms and the water. Cover the pan, bring to the boil, then lower the heat and simmer for 15 minutes.

4 Add the beans and cook, uncovered, for 5 minutes. With a slotted spoon, remove the vegetables to a warmed serving dish and keep hot.

5 Allow the cooking liquid to bubble up until it has reduced a little. Season with salt and pepper to taste, then stir in the yogurt, double cream and garam masala. Pour the sauce over the vegetables and garnish with fresh coriander. Serve with boiled rice and poppadums.

Madras Sambal

There are many variations of this popular dish but it is regularly cooked in one form or another in almost every south-Indian home. You can use any combination of vegetables that are in season.

Serves 4

225g/8oz/1 cup tuvar dhal or
  red split lentils
600ml/1 pint/2½ cups water
2.5ml/½ tsp ground turmeric
2 large potatoes, cut into
  2.5cm/1in chunks

30ml/2 tbsp oil
2.5ml/½ tsp black
  mustard seeds
1.5ml/¼ tsp fenugreek
  seeds
4 curry leaves
1 onion, thinly sliced
115g/4oz green beans, cut into
  2.5cm/1in lengths
5ml/1 tsp salt
2.5ml/½ tsp chilli powder
15ml/1 tbsp lemon juice
toasted coconut,
  to garnish
fresh coriander relish,
  to serve

1 Wash the tuvar dhal or lentils in several changes of water. Place in a heavy pan with the measured water and the turmeric. Bring to the boil, then reduce the heat, cover the pan with a tight-fitting lid and simmer for 30–35 minutes until the lentils are soft.

2 Par-boil the potatoes in a large pan of boiling water for 10 minutes. Drain well and set aside.

3 Heat the oil in a large frying pan and fry the mustard and fenugreek seeds and the curry leaves for 2–3 minutes until the seeds begin to splutter.

4 Add the sliced onion and the green beans to the pan and stir-fry for around 7–8 minutes. Add the par-boiled potatoes to the pan and cook for a further 2 minutes.

5 Drain the lentils. Stir them into the spiced potato mixture with the salt, chilli powder and lemon juice. Simmer for around 2 minutes or until everything is heated through. Garnish with the toasted coconut and serve with a freshly made coriander relish.

Vegetable Korma Energy 381kcal/1577kJ; Protein 5.1g; Carbohydrate 20.9g, of which sugars 9.9g; Fat 31.4g, of which saturates 19.3g; Cholesterol 78mg; Calcium 95mg; Fibre 3.9g; Sodium 108mg.
Madras Sambal Energy 401kcal/1687kJ; Protein 16.7g; Carbohydrate 50.8g, of which sugars 5.1g; Fat 16g, of which saturates 8.9g; Cholesterol 0mg; Calcium 52mg; Fibre 6.7g; Sodium 36mg.

Karahi Potatoes with Whole Spices

The potato is transformed into something quite exotic when it is cooked like this.

Serves 4

15ml/1 tbsp oil
5ml/1 tsp cumin seeds
3 curry leaves
5ml/1 tsp crushed dried
  red chillies
2.5ml/½ tsp mixed onion,
  mustard and fenugreek seeds

2.5ml/½ tsp fennel seeds
3 garlic cloves, sliced
2.5cm/1in piece fresh root
  ginger, grated
2 onions, sliced
6 new potatoes, thinly sliced
15ml/1 tbsp chopped fresh
  coriander (cilantro)
1 fresh red chilli, seeded
  and sliced
1 fresh green chilli, seeded
  and sliced

1 Heat the oil in a karahi, wok or heavy pan. Lower the heat slightly and add the cumin seeds, curry leaves, dried red chillies, mixed onion, mustard and fenugreek seeds, fennel seeds, garlic slices and ginger. Fry for 1 minute.

2 Add the onions and fry for a further 5 minutes, or until the onions are golden brown.

3 Add the potatoes, fresh coriander and sliced fresh red and green chillies and mix well. Cover the pan tightly with a lid or foil; if using foil, make sure that it does not touch the food. Cook over a very low heat for about 7 minutes or until the potatoes are tender.

4 Remove the pan from the heat, and take off the lid or foil cover. Serve hot straight from the pan.

> **Cook's Tip**
> *Try and choose a waxy variety of new potato for this fairly spicy vegetable dish; if you use a very soft potato, it will crumble and not be possible to cut it into thin slices without it breaking up. Suitable varieties are often labelled 'salad potatoes' when sold at supermarkets. Leave the skin on for an even tastier result.*

Indian Mee Goreng

This is a truly international noodle dish combining Indian, Chinese and Western ingredients. It is a delicious treat for lunch or supper, or any time of day.

Serves 4

450g/1lb fresh yellow
  egg noodles
60–90ml/4–6 tbsp
  vegetable oil
115g/4oz fried tofu or 150g/5oz
  firm tofu
2 eggs

30ml/2 tbsp water
salt and ground black pepper
1 onion, sliced
1 garlic clove, crushed
15ml/1 tbsp light soy sauce
30–45ml/2–3 tbsp
  tomato ketchup
15ml/1 tbsp chilli sauce
1 large cooked potato,
  evenly diced
4 spring onions
  (scallions), shredded
1–2 fresh green chillies,
  seeded and thinly
  sliced (optional)

1 Bring a large pan of water to the boil, add the fresh egg noodles and cook for just 2 minutes. Drain the noodles, rinse under cold water, drain again and set aside.

2 If using fried tofu, cut each cube in half, refresh it in a pan of boiling water, then drain well and set aside. Heat 30ml/ 2 tbsp of the oil in a large frying pan. If using plain tofu, cube it, fry until brown, then set aside.

3 Beat the eggs with 30ml/2 tbsp water and seasoning. Add to the frying pan and cook, without stirring, until set. Flip over, cook the other side, then slide it out of the pan, roll up and slice thinly.

4 Heat the remaining oil in a wok and fry the onion and garlic for 2–3 minutes. Add the drained noodles, soy sauce, ketchup and chilli sauce. Toss well over medium heat for 2 minutes, then add the diced potato. Reserve a few spring onion shreds for garnish and stir the rest into the noodles with the chilli, if using, and the tofu.

5 When hot, stir in the omelette slices. Serve on a hot platter, garnished with the remaining spring onion.

Karahi Potatoes Energy 152kcal/641kJ; Protein 3.8g; Carbohydrate 27.5g, of which sugars 6g; Fat 3.9g, of which saturates 0.5g; Cholesterol 0mg; Calcium 46mg; Fibre 2.6g; Sodium 19mg.
Mee Goreng Energy 478kcal/2010kJ; Protein 16.8g; Carbohydrate 64.2g, of which sugars 5.1g; Fat 18.9g, of which saturates 3.2g; Cholesterol 86mg; Calcium 323mg; Fibre 2.9g; Sodium 466mg.

Mung Beans with Potatoes

Small mung beans are one of the quicker-cooking pulses. They do not require soaking and are easy and convenient to use. In this recipe they are cooked with potatoes and Indian spices to give a tasty and nutritious dish.

Serves 4

175g/6oz/1 cup mung beans
750ml/1¼ pints/3 cups water
225g/8oz potatoes, cut into
　2cm/¾in chunks
30ml/2 tbsp oil
2.5ml/½ tsp cumin seeds
1 fresh green chilli,
　finely chopped
1 garlic clove, crushed
2.5cm/1in piece fresh root
　ginger, finely chopped
1.5ml/¼ tsp ground turmeric
2.5ml/½ tsp chilli powder
5ml/1 tsp salt
5ml/1 tsp sugar
4 curry leaves
5 tomatoes, peeled and
　finely chopped
15ml/1 tbsp tomato
　purée (paste)
curry leaves, to garnish
plain rice, to serve

1 Wash the beans. Pour the water into a pan, add the beans and bring to the boil. Boil hard for 15 minutes, then reduce the heat, cover the pan and simmer until soft, about 30 minutes cooking time. Drain.

2 In a separate pan, par-boil the chunks of potato in boiling water for about 10 minutes, until just tender, then drain well and put aside.

3 Heat the oil in a heavy pan and fry the cumin seeds until they splutter. Add the chilli, garlic and ginger, and fry for 3–4 minutes.

4 Add the turmeric, chilli powder, salt and sugar, and cook for 2 minutes, stirring to prevent the mixture from sticking to the pan.

5 Add the four curry leaves, chopped tomatoes and tomato purée, and simmer for about 5 minutes until the sauce has thickened. Mix the tomato sauce and the potatoes with the mung beans and heat through. Garnish with the extra curry leaves and serve with plain boiled rice.

Potatoes in a Fiery Red Sauce

This piquant potato dish should be hot and sour but, if you prefer a little less fire, you can reduce the chillies and add extra tomato purée instead. Likewise if you like your food with a kick, you can increase the number of dried chillies used.

Serves 4 to 6

450g/1lb small new potatoes,
　washed and dried
25g/1oz whole dried red chillies,
　preferably kashmiri
5ml/1½ tsp cumin seeds
4 garlic cloves
90ml/6 tbsp vegetable oil
60ml/4 tbsp thick tamarind juice
30ml/2 tbsp tomato
　purée (paste)
4 curry leaves
5ml/1 tsp sugar
1.5ml/¼ tsp asafoetida
salt
coriander (cilantro) leaves and
　lemon wedges, to garnish

1 Put the potatoes in a large pan. Add water to cover and bring to the boil. Add salt, then simmer for about 15 minutes, or until the potatoes are tender, but do not let them get too soft. To test, insert a thin sharp knife into the potatoes. It should slip off cleanly when the potatoes are fully cooked through. Drain thoroughly and leave to cool.

2 Soak the chillies for 5 minutes in a bowl of warm water. Drain well and grind them with the cumin seeds and garlic cloves to a coarse paste using a mortar and pestle. Alternatively, purée the ingredients in a blender or food processor.

3 Fry the paste, tamarind juice, tomato purée, curry leaves, salt, sugar and asafoetida until the oil separates. Add the potatoes. Reduce the heat, cover and simmer for about 10 minutes. Garnish with coriander and lemon wedges and serve immediately.

Cook's Tip
Asafoetida is a pungent spice and can seem overpowering in its raw state, but once it has been added to a dish and cooked, it imparts a deep oniony flavour.

Mung Beans Energy 265kcal/1118kJ; Protein 13.8g; Carbohydrate 37.4g, of which sugars 5.7g; Fat 7.9g, of which saturates 1.1g; Cholesterol 0mg; Calcium 58mg; Fibre 5.8g; Sodium 34mg.
Potatoes in a Fiery Sauce Energy 156kcal/650kJ; Protein 1.7g; Carbohydrate 12.8g, of which sugars 1.7g; Fat 11.3g, of which saturates 1.4g; Cholesterol 0mg; Calcium 8mg; Fibre 0.9g; Sodium 21mg.

Stuffed Baby Vegetables

The combination of potatoes and aubergines is popular in Indian cooking.

Serves 4
12 small potatoes
8 baby aubergines (eggplants)

For the stuffing
15ml/1 tbsp sesame seeds
30ml/2 tbsp ground coriander
30ml/2 tbsp ground cumin
2.5ml/½ tsp salt
1.5ml/¼ tsp chilli powder
2.5ml/½ tsp ground turmeric
10ml/2 tsp sugar

1.5ml/¼ tsp garam masala
15ml/1 tbsp gram flour
2 garlic cloves, crushed
15ml/1 tbsp lemon juice
30ml/2 tbsp chopped fresh
 coriander (cilantro)

For the sauce
15ml/1 tbsp oil
2.5ml/½ tsp black
 mustard seeds
400g/14oz can
 chopped tomatoes
30ml/2 tbsp chopped fresh
 coriander (cilantro)
150ml/¼ pint/⅔ cup water

1 Preheat the oven to 200°C/400°F/Gas 6. Make deep slits in the potatoes and aubergines to hold the stuffing, ensuring that you do not cut right through.

2 Mix all the ingredients for the stuffing together in a large mixing bowl.

3 Carefully spoon the spicy stuffing mixture into each of the slits in the potatoes and aubergines.

4 Arrange the stuffed potatoes and aubergines in a greased ovenproof dish, filling side up.

5 For the sauce, heat the oil in a heavy pan and fry the mustard seeds for 2 minutes until they begin to splutter, then add the canned tomatoes, chopped coriander and any leftover stuffing. Stir in the water. Bring to the boil and simmer for 5 minutes until the sauce thickens.

6 Pour the tomato sauce over the potatoes and aubergines. Cover and bake in the oven for 25–30 minutes until the potatoes and aubergines are soft.

Lentils and Rice with Potatoes

Here, lentils are cooked with whole and ground spices, potato, rice and onion to produce a tasty and nutritious meal.

Serves 4
150g/5oz/¾ cup tuvar dhal or
 red split lentils

115g/4oz/½ cup basmati rice
1 large potato
1 large onion
30ml/2 tbsp oil
4 whole cloves
1.5ml/¼ tsp cumin seeds
1.5ml/¼ tsp ground turmeric
10ml/2 tsp salt
300ml/½ pint/1¼ cups water

1 Wash the tuvar dhal or red split lentils and rice in several changes of cold water. Put into a bowl and cover with water. Leave to soak for 15 minutes, then transfer to a strainer and drain well.

2 Peel the potato, then cut it into 2.5cm/1in chunks. Using a sharp knife, thinly slice the onion and set aside for later.

3 Heat the oil in a heavy pan and fry the cloves and cumin seeds for 2 minutes until the seeds are beginning to splutter.

4 Add the onion and potato chunks and fry for 5 minutes. Stir in the lentils, rice, turmeric and salt and cook for a further 3 minutes.

5 Add the water. Bring to the boil, cover and simmer gently for 15–20 minutes until all the water has been absorbed and the potato chunks are tender. Leave to stand, covered, for about 10 minutes before serving.

> **Cook's Tip**
> *Red split lentils are very economical and are widely available in most supermarkets. Before cooking they are salmon-coloured and they turn a pale, dull yellow during cooking. They have a mild, pleasant, nutty flavour. Soaking them in water overnight rehydrates the lentils and speeds up the cooking process but is not strictly necessary.*

Stuffed Baby Vegetables Energy 222kcal/938kJ; Protein 6.5g; Carbohydrate 35.3g, of which sugars 6.6g; Fat 7.3g, of which saturates 1.2g; Cholesterol 0mg; Calcium 72mg; Fibre 4.4g; Sodium 31mg.
Lentils and Rice Energy 364kcal/1529kJ; Protein 13.3g; Carbohydrate 57.8g, of which sugars 4.4g; Fat 9.8g, of which saturates 1.4g; Cholesterol 0mg; Calcium 49mg; Fibre 3g; Sodium 22mg.

Malay Vegetable Curry with Cumin and Turmeric

Originally from southern India, this delicious spicy dish is substantial and flexible – although delicious with sweet potato, feel free to choose your own assortment of vegetables, such as pumpkin, butternut squash, winter melon, yams, aubergines or beans.

Serves 4

2–3 green chillies, seeded and chopped
25g/1oz fresh root ginger, peeled and chopped
5–10ml/1–2 tsp roasted cumin seeds
10ml/2 tsp sugar
5–10ml/1–2 tsp ground turmeric
1 cinnamon stick
5ml/1 tsp salt
2 carrots, cut into bitesize sticks
2 sweet potatoes, cut into bitesize sticks
2 courgettes (zucchini), partially peeled in strips, seeded and cut into bitesize sticks
1 green plantain, peeled and cut into bitesize sticks
small coil of long (snake) beans or a handful of green beans, cut into bitesize sticks
handful fresh curry leaves
1 fresh coconut, grated
250ml/8fl oz/1 cup natural (plain) yogurt
salt and ground black pepper

1 Using a mortar and pestle or a food processor, grind the chillies, ginger, roasted cumin seeds and sugar to a paste.

2 In a heavy pan, bring 450ml/15fl oz/scant 2 cups water to the boil. Stir in the turmeric, cinnamon stick and salt. Add the carrots and cook for 1 minute. Add the sweet potatoes and cook for 2 minutes. Add the courgettes, plantain and beans and cook for a further 2 minutes. Reduce the heat, stir in the spice paste and curry leaves, and cook gently for 4–5 minutes, or until the vegetables are tender but not soft and mushy, and the liquid has greatly reduced.

3 Gently stir in half the coconut. Take the pan off the heat and fold in the yogurt. Season to taste with salt and pepper. Quickly roast the remaining coconut in a heavy pan over a high heat, until nicely browned. Sprinkle a little over the vegetables, and serve the rest separately.

Cauliflower and Potatoes Chilli-style

Cauliflower and potatoes are encrusted with Indian spices in this delicious recipe. It is a popular side dish or can be served as a main course with other dishes such as a salad, dhal or simply with Indian breads.

Serves 4

450g/1lb potatoes, cut into 2.5 cm/1 in chunks
30ml/2 tbsp oil
5ml/1 tsp cumin seeds
1 green chilli, finely chopped
450g/1lb cauliflower, broken into florets
5ml/1 tsp ground coriander
5ml/1 tsp ground cumin
1.5ml/1/4 tsp chilli powder
2.5ml/1/2 tsp ground turmeric
2.5ml/1/2 tsp salt
chopped fresh coriander (cilantro), to garnish
tomato and onion salad and pickle, to serve

1 Par-boil the potatoes in a large pan of boiling water for 10 minutes. Drain well and set aside.

2 Heat the oil in a wok or large frying pan and fry the cumin seeds for about 2 minutes until they begin to splutter and release their fragrance. Add the chilli to the pan and fry, stirring constantly, for a further 1 minute.

3 Add the cauliflower florets to the pan and fry, stirring constantly, for 5 minutes.

4 Add the potatoes and the ground spices and salt and cook for 7–10 minutes, or until both the vegetables are tender.

5 Garnish with fresh coriander and serve with a tomato and onion salad and pickle.

Variation
Try using sweet potatoes instead of ordinary potatoes for an alternative curry with a sweeter flavour. The cauliflower could also be replaced with the same amount of broccoli.

Malay Curry Energy 419kcal/1753kJ; Protein 9.9g; Carbohydrate 47.7g, of which sugars 19.4g; Fat 23g, of which saturates 16.9g; Cholesterol 0mg; Calcium 176mg; Fibre 9g; Sodium 104mg.
Cauliflower Chilli-style Energy 181kcal/759kJ; Protein 6.7g; Carbohydrate 23.2g, of which sugars 4.3g; Fat 7.5g, of which saturates 1.1g; Cholesterol 0mg; Calcium 40mg; Fibre 3.2g; Sodium 24mg.

Curried Spinach and Potato with Mixed Chillies

This delicious spinach and potato curry, suitable for vegetarians, is mildly spiced with a warming flavour from the fresh and dried chillies.

Serves 4 to 6
60ml/4 tbsp vegetable oil
225g/8oz potato
2.5cm/1in piece fresh root
　ginger, crushed
4 garlic cloves, crushed
1 onion, coarsely chopped
2 green chillies, chopped
2 whole dried red chillies,
　coarsely broken
5ml/1 tsp cumin seeds
225g/8oz fresh spinach, trimmed,
　washed and chopped or
　225g/8oz frozen spinach,
　thawed and drained
salt
2 firm tomatoes, coarsely
　chopped, to garnish

1 Wash the potatoes and cut into quarters. If using small new potatoes, leave them whole. Heat the oil in a frying pan and fry the potatoes until brown on all sides. Remove and set aside.

2 Remove the excess oil leaving 15ml/1 tbsp in the pan. Fry the ginger, garlic, onion, green chillies, dried chillies and cumin seeds until the onion is golden brown.

3 Add the potatoes and salt to the pan and stir well. Cover the pan and cook gently until the potatoes are tender and can be easily pierced with a sharp knife.

4 Add the spinach and stir well. Cook with the pan uncovered until the spinach is tender and all the excess fluids in the pan have evaporated. Transfer the curry to a serving plate, garnish with the chopped tomatoes and serve immediately.

Cook's Tip
India is blessed with over 18 varieties of spinach. If you have access to an Indian or Chinese grocer, look out for some of the more unusual varieties.

Chinese Potatoes with Chilli Beans

East meets West in this American-style dish with a distinctly Chinese flavour – the sauce is very tasty. Try it as a quick supper when you fancy a potato recipe with a little zing.

Serves 4
4 medium firm or waxy potatoes,
　cut into thick chunks
30ml/2 tbsp sunflower or
　groundnut (peanut) oil
3 spring onions (scallions), sliced
1 large fresh chilli, seeded
　and sliced
2 garlic cloves, crushed
400g/14oz can red kidney
　beans, drained
30ml/2 tbsp soy sauce
15ml/1 tbsp sesame oil
salt and ground black pepper
15ml/1 tbsp sesame seeds,
　to garnish
chopped fresh coriander (cilantro)
　or parsley, to garnish

1 Cook the potatoes in boiling water until they are just tender. Take care not to overcook them. Drain and reserve.

2 Heat the oil in a large frying pan or wok over a medium-high heat. Add the spring onions and chilli to the pan and stir-fry for about 1 minute, then add the garlic and stir-fry for a few seconds longer.

3 Add the potatoes, stirring well, then the beans and finally the soy sauce and sesame oil.

4 Season to taste with salt and ground black pepper and continue to cook the vegetables until they are well heated through. Sprinkle with the sesame seeds and the coriander or parsley and serve hot.

Cook's Tip
If you prefer your food with a little more heat, then simply add in an extra chopped chilli pepper. Alternatively, replace the sunflower or groundnut (peanut) oil with some oil that has been flavoured with chillies.

Curried Spinach Energy 135kcal/560kJ; Protein 3g; Carbohydrate 13.5g, of which sugars 5.9g; Fat 8g, of which saturates 1g; Cholesterol 0mg; Calcium 86mg; Fibre 2.6g; Sodium 62mg.
Chinese Potatoes Energy 272kcal/1141kJ; Protein 9.7g; Carbohydrate 34.8g, of which sugars 5.7g; Fat 11.4g, of which saturates 1.6g; Cholesterol 0mg; Calcium 107mg; Fibre 7.6g; Sodium 936mg.

Baked Jacket Potatoes

Once the potato, one of England's staple foods, is cooked in its skin in the oven it is transformed into the ultimate comfort food. The deliciously crispy skin masks a moreishly soft and fluffy interior. It can be served split and laced with butter or sour cream, or with a filling of grated cheese.

Serves 4
4 large floury potatoes of even size, such as King Edward or Maris Piper
a little oil
salt (optional)
butter or sour cream, to serve
chopped fresh parsley or chives, to serve

1 Preheat the oven to 200°C/400°F/Gas 6. Scrub and dry the potatoes, and prick the skins with a fork to prevent them bursting during cooking.

2 Rub the skins all over with a little oil and sprinkle with a little salt, if using.

3 Put the potatoes in the hot oven, either on a baking sheet or straight on to the oven shelf. Cook for about 1 hour or until soft throughout.

4 Leave the cooked potatoes to stand for 5 minutes before splitting them open. Be careful of the escaping steam.

5 Serve with a dollop of butter on top, or sour cream and a sprinkling of parsley or chives.

> **Cook's Tips**
> • *Cooking potatoes in the microwave is quicker and easier, but the results will be nowhere near as good. If you have the time to prepare baked potatoes as laid out above it is well worth the effort.*
> • *Ensure that the potatoes are completely cooked by inserting a sharp knife or a metal skewer into the centre of the potato. You will be able to tell if they need cooking a bit longer because there will be a little resistance.*

Roast Potatoes

For crisp roasties with fluffy interiors, cook them in a single layer. Shaking the parboiled potatoes to roughen the edges will ensure deliciously crispy results.

Serves 4
1.3kg/3lb floury potatoes
90ml/6 tbsp vegetable oil

1 Preheat the oven to 200°C/400°F/Gas 6. Peel the potatoes and cut into chunks. Boil in salted water for 5 minutes, drain, return to the pan, and shake them to roughen the surfaces.

2 Put the oil into a large roasting pan and put into the hot oven to heat. Add the potatoes, coating them in the oil. Return to the oven and roast for 40–50 minutes, turning once or twice, until crisp, golden and cooked through.

Chips

Chips, or French fries, are the ultimate potato classic. Fry these twice – once to cook them, and the second time to crisp them.

Serves 4
sunflower or vegetable oil, for deep frying
675g/1½lb potatoes
salt

1 Heat the oil to 150°C/300°F. Peel the potatoes and cut them into chips (French fries) about 1cm/½in thick. Rinse and dry.

2 Lower a batch of chips into the hot oil and cook for about 5 minutes or until tender but not browned. Lift out on to kitchen paper and leave to cool.

3 Just before serving, increase the temperature of the oil to 190°C/375°F. Add the par-cooked chips, in batches. Cook until crisp and golden.

4 Lift out of the fryer and drain on kitchen paper. Sprinkle the cooked chips with salt and serve immediately.

Baked Jacket Potatoes Energy 182kcal/772kJ; Protein 3.8g; Carbohydrate 36.2g, of which sugars 2.9g; Fat 3.4g, of which saturates 0.6g; Cholesterol 0mg; Calcium 14mg; Fibre 2.3g; Sodium 25mg.
Roast Potatoes Energy 484kcal/2048kJ; Protein 9.4g; Carbohydrate 84.2g, of which sugars 2g; Fat 14.6g, of which saturates 5.9g; Cholesterol 13mg; Calcium 26mg; Fibre 5.9g; Sodium 29mg.
Chips Energy 403kcal/1689kJ; Protein 5.4g; Carbohydrate 51.5g, of which sugars 2.9g; Fat 14.5g, of which saturates 6.1g; Cholesterol 0mg; Calcium 19mg; Fibre 3.7g; Sodium 59mg.

Griddle Potatoes

This dish makes a tasty accompaniment to grilled or barbecued vegetables.

Serves 4–6

2 onions, peeled and chopped

450–675g/1lb–1½lb whole cooked potatoes, boiled in their skins

a mixture of butter and oil, for shallow frying

salt and ground black pepper

I Put the onions in a large pan and scald them briefly in boiling water. Refresh under cold water and drain well. Peel and slice the potatoes.

2 Put a mixture of butter and oil into a large, heavy frying pan and heat well. When the fat is hot, fry the onion until tender. Add the potato slices and brown them together, turning the potato slices to brown as evenly as possible on both sides. Transfer to a warmed serving dish and season with salt and pepper. Serve very hot.

Garlicky Roasties

Potatoes roasted in their skins retain a deep, earthy taste while the garlic mellows on cooking.

60–75ml/4–5 tbsp sunflower oil

10ml/2 tsp walnut oil

2 whole garlic bulbs, unpeeled

salt

Serves 4

1kg/2¼lb small floury potatoes

I Preheat the oven to 240°C/475°F/Gas 9. Place the potatoes in a pan of cold water and bring to the boil. Drain.

2 Combine the oils in a roasting pan and place in the oven to get really hot. Add the potatoes and garlic and coat in oil.

3 Sprinkle with salt and roast for 10 minutes. Reduce the heat to 200°C/400°F/Gas 6. Continue roasting, basting occasionally, for 40 minutes. Serve with several cloves of garlic per portion.

Hasselback Potatoes

This dish is named after the Stockholm restaurant that created it, and is a method of cooking rather than a recipe. Choose similar-sized potatoes so that they cook uniformly, and the essential thing is to cut the potatoes most of the way, but not completely, through. It is a good idea to thread a skewer through the potato three-quarters of the way down before cutting, so that your knife travels just to the point you want it to reach and no farther.

Serves 4

4 large potatoes

75g/3oz/6 tbsp butter

45ml/3 tbsp olive oil

50g/2oz/1 cup fine fresh breadcrumbs

50g/2oz/⅔ cup grated Parmesan cheese

salt and ground black pepper

I Preheat the oven to 200°C/400°F/Gas 6. Peel the potatoes, then – and this is the crucial part – cut them widthways, not lengthways, down to three-quarters of their depth at 3mm/⅛in intervals, preferably at a slight angle.

2 Wash the potatoes in cold water, then arrange, cut sides uppermost, in a deep, ovenproof dish.

3 Melt the butter in a small pan, then add the olive oil and mix together. Brush the mixture over the potatoes, then season well with salt and black pepper. Sprinkle over the breadcrumbs and the grated cheese.

4 Roast the potatoes in the preheated oven for about 1 hour, depending on their size, until golden brown and fanned apart along the cut lines. Serve hot.

Cook's Tip

If you are using very large potatoes then it will shorten the cooking time if you parboil them briefly before roasting. Do not move them around in the oven while they roast, because they won't crisp up properly.

Hasselback Potatoes Energy 380kcal/1593kJ; Protein 9.9g; Carbohydrate 42g, of which sugars 3.1g; Fat 20.4g, of which saturates 12.5g; Cholesterol 52mg; Calcium 182mg; Fibre 2.3g; Sodium 367mg.
Griddle Potatoes Energy 163kcal/681kJ; Protein 3.4g; Carbohydrate 26.4g, of which sugars 5g; Fat 5.5g, of which saturates 3.3g; Cholesterol 13mg; Calcium 26mg; Fibre 2.6g; Sodium 49mg.
Garlicky Roasties Energy 312kcal/1310kJ; Protein 6.2g; Carbohydrate 44.3g, of which sugars 3.7g; Fat 13.4g, of which saturates 1.7g; Cholesterol 0mg; Calcium 20mg; Fibre 3.5g; Sodium 29mg.

Chilli Fried Potatoes

These make the perfect accompaniment for eggs and cheese, and also go very well with vegetarian chilli.

Serves 4

6 fresh jalapeño chillies
60ml/4 tbsp vegetable oil
1 onion, finely chopped
450g/1lb waxy potatoes, scrubbed
    and cut in 1cm/½ in cubes
few sprigs of fresh oregano,
    chopped, plus extra sprigs,
    to garnish
75g/3oz/1 cup freshly grated
    Parmesan cheese (optional)

1 Dry roast the jalapeños in a griddle pan, turning them frequently so that the skins blacken but do not burn. Place them in a strong plastic bag and tie the top to keep the steam in. Set aside for 20 minutes.

2 Remove the jalapeños from the bag, peel off their skins and remove any stems. Cut them in half, carefully scrape out the seeds, then chop the flesh finely.

3 Meanwhile, heat half the oil in a large heavy frying pan which has a lid. Add the onion and fry, stirring occasionally, for about 3–4 minutes, until translucent, then add the potato cubes.

4 Stir to coat the potato cubes in oil, then cover the pan and cook over a moderate heat for 20–25 minutes, until the potatoes are tender. Shake the pan occasionally to stop them from sticking to the bottom.

5 When the potatoes are tender, push them to the side of the frying pan, then add the remaining oil.

6 When the oil is hot, spread out the potatoes again and add the chopped jalapeños. Cook over a high heat for 5–10 minutes, stirring carefully so that the potatoes turn golden brown all over but do not break up.

7 Add the chopped oregano, with the grated Parmesan, if using. Mix gently, spoon on to a heated serving dish and garnish with extra oregano sprigs. Serve as part of a cooked breakfast or brunch.

Oven Chip Roasties

This easy alternative to deep-fried chips (French fries) tastes just as good and is much easier to cook, as well as being healthier for you.

Serves 4–6

150ml/¼ pint/⅔ cup olive oil
4 medium to large
    baking potatoes
5ml/1 tsp mixed dried
    herbs (optional)
sea salt flakes
mayonnaise, to serve

1 Preheat the oven to the highest temperature, which is generally 240°C/475°F/Gas 9. Lightly oil a large shallow roasting pan and place it in the oven to get really hot while you prepare the potatoes.

2 Cut the potatoes in half lengthways, then into long thin wedges, or thicker ones, if you prefer. Brush each side lightly with olive oil.

3 When the oven is really hot, remove the pan carefully and sprinkle the potato wedges over it, spreading them out in a single layer over the hot oil.

4 Sprinkle the potato wedges with the herbs and salt and roast for about 20 minutes, or longer if they are thicker, until they are golden brown, crisp and lightly puffy. Remove from the oven and serve with a dollop of mayonnaise.

Cook's Tip
Oven chip roasties make great mid-week suppers served with fried eggs, mushrooms and tomatoes.

Variation
Sweet potatoes also make fine oven chips. Prepare and roast in the same way as above, although you may find they do not take as long to cook.

Chilli Potatoes Energy 186kcal/775kJ; Protein 2.5g; Carbohydrate 19.4g, of which sugars 2.4g; Fat 11.4g, of which saturates 1.4g; Cholesterol 0mg; Calcium 14mg; Fibre 1.3g; Sodium 14mg.
Oven Chip Roasties Energy 200kcal/838kJ; Protein 3.2g; Carbohydrate 28g, of which sugars 2.2g; Fat 9.1g, of which saturates 1.4g; Cholesterol 0mg; Calcium 15mg; Fibre 1.7g; Sodium 19mg.

Rosemary and Garlic New Potatoes

These new potatoes, flavoured with fresh rosemary and lots of garlic, are an ideal accompaniment to vegetable stews.

5 garlic cloves, peeled and bruised
3 sprigs of rosemary
30ml/2 tbsp olive oil
sea salt and ground black pepper

Serves 4
800g/1¾lb small new potatoes

1 Preheat the oven to 200°C/400°F/Gas 6. Put the potatoes, garlic and rosemary in a roasting pan. Drizzle with the olive oil, and toss to coat the ingredients evenly in the oil. Season well with salt and pepper.

2 Bake the potatoes in the preheated oven for about 40–45 minutes until the potatoes are crisp on the outside and soft in the centre. Remove the pan from the oven halfway through cooking and give it a shake to turn the potatoes and coat them in oil.

3 Test the potatoes are done by inserting the tip of a knife or a metal skewer into the centre of a couple of potatoes. Discard the rosemary and garlic, if you wish, and serve hot.

Variations
• Shallots can be roasted in the same way. Cook for 35 minutes or until tender. Roast a pan of shallots on their own or add a handful in with the potatoes.
• Add a handful of sweet vine-ripened cherry tomatoes to the roasting pan before baking for a delicious Mediterranean twist.

Cook's Tip
So much can be said about the healing power of garlic. It is particularly valued for its ability to boost the immune system, helping to protect us against disease.

Kailkenny Cabbage and Potatoes

This cabbage and potato dish is ideal alongside any main course.

50g/2oz/¼ cup butter
50ml/2fl oz/¼ cup milk
450g/1lb cabbage, finely shredded
30ml/2 tbsp olive oil
50ml/2fl oz/¼ cup double (heavy) cream
salt and ground black pepper

Serves 4
450g/1lb potatoes, peeled and chopped

1 Boil the potatoes for 15–20 minutes. Drain, replace on the heat for a few minutes, then mash. Heat the butter and milk in a pan and then mix into the mashed potatoes. Season to taste.

2 Heat the olive oil in a large frying pan, add the shredded cabbage and fry for a few minutes. Season to taste. Add the potato, mix well, then stir in the cream. Serve immediately.

Easy Mashed Potatoes

These mashed potatoes are the ideal accompaniment to vegetarian sausages.

about 150ml/¼pint/⅔ cup milk
115g/4oz/½ cup soft butter
salt
freshly grated nutmeg (optional)

Serves 4
1kg/2¼lb floury potatoes, such as Maris Piper

1 Peel the potatoes and cook them whole in a large pan of boiling water for about 20 minutes or until soft throughout. Drain. Warm the milk and butter in a large pan.

2 Push the warm potatoes through a ricer, pass them through a mouli, or mash with a potato masher or fork.

3 Add the mashed potato to the milk and beat with a wooden spoon, adding extra milk if necessary to achieve the desired consistency. Season to taste with salt and a little grated nutmeg, if using. Serve immediately.

Rosemary and Garlic Potatoes Energy 171kcal/721kJ; Protein 3.9g; Carbohydrate 31.8g, of which sugars 2.9g; Fat 3.9g, of which saturates 0.7g; Cholesterol 0mg; Calcium 41mg; Fibre 2.8g; Sodium 26mg.
Kailkenny Energy 183kcal/766kJ; Protein 3.9g; Carbohydrate 24g, of which sugars 7.3g; Fat 8.5g, of which saturates 2.4g; Cholesterol 7mg; Calcium 73mg; Fibre 3.5g; Sodium 24mg.
Easy Mashed Potatoes Energy 338kcal/1424kJ; Protein 5.9g; Carbohydrate 50.4g, of which sugars 3.3g; Fat 14g, of which saturates 9.1g; Cholesterol 39mg; Calcium 42mg; Fibre 3.6g; Sodium 140mg.

Fennel, Potato and Garlic Mash

This flavoursome mash of potato, fennel and garlic goes particularly well with warming winter stews.

Serves 4
1 head of garlic, separated into cloves
800g/1¾lb boiling potatoes, cut into chunks
2 large fennel bulbs
65g/2½oz/5 tbsp butter or 90ml/6 tbsp extra virgin olive oil
120–150ml/4–5fl oz/½–⅔ cup milk or single (light) cream
freshly grated nutmeg
salt and ground black pepper

1 If using a food mill to mash the potato, leave the garlic unpeeled, otherwise peel it. Boil the garlic and potatoes in salted water for 20 minutes.

2 Meanwhile, trim and roughly chop the fennel, reserving any feathery tops. Chop the tops and set them aside.

3 Heat 25g/1oz/2 tbsp of the butter or 30ml/2 tbsp of the oil in a heavy pan. Add the fennel, cover and cook over a low heat for 20–30 minutes, until soft but not browned.

4 Drain and mash the potatoes and garlic. Purée the fennel in a food mill or blender and beat it into the potato with the remaining butter or olive oil.

5 Warm the milk or cream and beat into the potato and fennel to make a creamy mixture. Season and add a little grated nutmeg.

6 Reheat gently, then beat in the reserved chopped fennel tops. Transfer to a warmed dish and serve immediately.

Cook's Tip
A food mill is good for mashing potatoes as it ensures a smooth texture. Never mash potatoes in a food processor or blender as this releases the starch, giving a result that resembles wallpaper paste.

Celeriac and Potato Purée

Celeriac is a delicious vegetable which is ignored too often. It is so excellent grated raw into salads or slowly roasted with a medley of other root vegetables. Here it is mixed with potato in a purée that makes an excellent alternative to traditional mashed potato.

Serves 4
1 celeriac bulb, cut into chunks
1 lemon
2 potatoes, cut into chunks
300ml/½ pint/1¼ cups double (heavy) cream
salt and ground black pepper
chopped chives, to garnish

1 Place the celeriac in a pan. Cut the lemon in half and squeeze it into the pan, dropping the two halves in too.

2 Add the potatoes to the pan and just cover with cold water. Place a disc of baking parchment over the vegetables. Bring to the boil, reduce the heat and simmer until the potatoes are tender, about 20 minutes.

3 Remove the lemon halves and drain through a colander. Return to the pan and allow to steam dry for a few minutes over a low heat.

4 Remove from the heat and purée in a food processor. Put this mixture aside until you need it, it can be kept in the refrigerator for a few days, covered with clear film (plastic wrap).

5 When ready to use, pour the cream into a pan and bring almost to the boil. Add the celeriac mixture and stir to heat through. Season with salt and ground black pepper, garnish wth chopped chives and serve.

Cook's Tip
This recipe makes a very light, creamy purée. Use less cream to achieve a firmer purée, more for a softer purée. Be sure the cream is almost boiling or it will cool the mixture. Keep the purée warm in a bowl over simmering water.

Fennel Mash Energy 144kcal/608kJ; Protein 4g; Carbohydrate 24.4g, of which sugars 4.6g; Fat 4.1g, of which saturates 2.3g; Cholesterol 10mg; Calcium 60mg; Fibre 4g; Sodium 61mg.
Celeriac Purée Energy 403kcal/1661kJ; Protein 2.2g; Carbohydrate 7.9g, of which sugars 2.3g; Fat 40.5g, of which saturates 25.1g; Cholesterol 103mg; Calcium 65mg; Fibre 1.1g; Sodium 58mg.

Garlic Mashed Potatoes

These creamy mashed potatoes are deliciously garlicky an make an ideal accompaniment to all kinds of vegetarian main dishes.

Serves 6–8

3 whole garlic bulbs, separated
   into cloves, unpeeled
115g/4oz/8 tbsp unsalted butter
1.5kg/3lb baking
   potatoes, quartered
about 120–175ml/4–6fl oz/
   ½–¾ cup milk
salt and ground white pepper

1 Bring a small pan of water to the boil over a high heat. Add two-thirds of the garlic cloves and boil for 2 minutes. Drain the pan and then peel the boiled garlic cloves.

2 Place the remaining garlic cloves in a roasting pan and bake in a preheated oven at 200°C/400°F/Gas 6 for 30–40 minutes.

3 In a heavy frying pan, melt 50g/2oz/4 tbsp of the butter over a low heat. Add the blanched garlic cloves, then cover and cook gently for 20–25 minutes until very tender and just golden, shaking the pan and stirring occasionally. Do not allow the garlic to scorch or brown.

4 Remove the pan from the heat and cool. Spoon the garlic and melted butter into a blender or a food processor fitted with the metal blade and process until smooth. Transfer into a bowl, press clear film (plastic wrap) on to the surface to prevent a skin forming and set aside.

5 Cook the potatoes in boiling salted water until tender, then drain and pass through a food mill or press through a sieve (strainer) back into the pan. Return the pan to a medium heat and, using a wooden spoon, stir the potatoes for 1–2 minutes to dry out completely. Remove the pan from the heat.

6 Warm the milk over a medium-high heat until bubbles form around the edge. Gradually beat the milk, remaining butter and garlic purée into the potatoes. Season with salt, if needed, and white pepper, and serve hot, with the roasted garlic cloves.

Potato and Spring Onion Champ

Simple but unbelievably tasty, this traditional Irish way with mashed potatoes makes an excellent companion for a hearty vegetarian stew.

Serves 4

900g/2lb floury potatoes
1 small bunch spring onions
   (scallions), finely chopped
150ml/¼ pint/⅔ cup milk
50g/2oz/¼ cup butter
salt and ground black pepper

1 Cut the potatoes up into large chunks and put them in a large pan. Add water to cover and bring to the boil. Add salt, then simmer for about 15 minutes, or until the potatoes are tender, but do not let them get too soft. Drain thoroughly and leave to cool.

2 Meanwhile, put the spring onions into a small pan with the milk. Bring the mixture gently to the boil, then reduce the heat to low and simmer very gently until the spring onions are just tender.

3 When the potatoes are cool enough to handle, peel and return to the pan. Place the pan back on the heat and, using a wooden spoon, stir gently and constantly for about 1 minute until any excess moisture has evaporated. Remove the pan from the heat.

4 Mash the potatoes thoroughly with the milk and spring onions and season with salt and ground black pepper. Serve hot with a pool of melted butter in each portion.

Cook's Tips
• *If you make too much mashed potato, don't worry. It will keep well in the refrigerator if covered, and then it simply needs re-heating before using.*
• *Evaporating the excess moisture from the potatoes before mashing ensures that you get light and airy mash.*

Garlic Mashed Potatoes Energy 261kcal/1093kJ; Protein 5g; Carbohydrate 33.3g, of which sugars 3.8g; Fat 12.8g, of which saturates 7.9g; Cholesterol 32mg; Calcium 43mg; Fibre 2.4g; Sodium 118mg.
Champ Energy 186kcal/790kJ; Protein 7.4g; Carbohydrate 37.2g, of which sugars 5.9g; Fat 2g, of which saturates 0.9g; Cholesterol 5mg; Calcium 121mg; Fibre 2.9g; Sodium 51mg.

Spiced Potato Purée

A flavoursome and fragrant addition to a festive dining table, this delicately spiced potato purée, originating from Holland, is the perfect accompaniment to any winter dinner and is especially delicious served alongside roasted onions.

Serves 4
750g/1lb 10oz peeled floury
    potatoes, cut into quarters
½ tsp salt
½ tsp paprika
½ tsp nutmeg
½ tsp black pepper
2 egg yolks
knob (pat) of butter
milk

1 Preheat the oven to 220°C/425°F/Gas 7. Grease an ovenproof dish with butter or line a baking sheet with baking parchment.

2 Put the potatoes in a pan, add water to cover, bring to the boil and cook for about 15 minutes, or until tender. Drain well.

3 While still warm, pass the potatoes through a potato ricer or alternatively, mash with a hand-held electric mixer, but take care as a mixer can produce a purée that is too sticky.

4 Stir in the salt, spices, egg yolks and butter. Add some milk if the purée seems too thick.

5 While still warm, pipe or spread the purée with a fork into the prepared dish. Alternatively, pipe rosettes on to the baking sheet lined with baking parchment.

6 Bake the purée in the oven for 20 minutes. When cooked, if unpiped, transfer the hot purée into a serving dish and place on the dining table. Allow people to serve themselves.

> **Variation**
> *This traditional side dish makes a warming and decadent meal in its own right if smothered in a rich cheese sauce and baked for around 20 minutes, until golden.*

Garlic Sweet Potato Mash

Delicious mashed with garlicky butter, orange-fleshed sweet potatoes not only look good, they're packed with vitamins.

40g/1½oz/3 tbsp unsalted butter
3 garlic cloves, crushed
salt and ground black pepper

Serves 4
4 large sweet potatoes, total
    weight about 900g/2lb, cubed

1 Put the sweet potatoes in a large pan. Add enough water to cover and bring to the boil. Add a little salt, then simmer for about 15 minutes, or until the potatoes are tender, but do not let them get too soft. Drain thoroughly in a colander and then return them to the pan.

2 Melt the butter in a heavy frying pan, then cook the garlic over a low to medium heat for about 1–2 minutes until it turns light golden. Stir the garlic frequently to prevent it from burning, otherwise it will taste bitter.

3 Pour the garlic butter over the sweet potatoes, season with salt and plenty of black pepper, and mash thoroughly until smooth and creamy. Serve immediately.

> **Variation**
> *Add some chopped fresh herbs, such as parsley or coriander (cilantro), if you wish.*

> **Cook's Tips**
> • *If the sweet potatoes seem to be on the dry side when you are mashing them, add a little milk.*
> • *Orange-fleshed sweet potatoes are rich in beta carotene and vitamins C and E, which are believed to be linked with lowering the risk of cancer, heart disease and strokes.*

Potato Purée Energy 174kcal/732kJ; Protein 4.5g; Carbohydrate 28.4g, of which sugars 2.3g; Fat 5.4g, of which saturates 2.3g; Cholesterol 106mg; Calcium 24mg; Fibre 1.8g; Sodium 236mg.
Sweet Potato Mash Energy 586kcal/2477kJ; Protein 16.3g; Carbohydrate 101.4g, of which sugars 52.1g; Fat 15.8g, of which saturates 7.1g; Cholesterol 240mg; Calcium 182mg; Fibre 2.8g; Sodium 968mg.

Masala Mashed Potatoes

This delightfully simple variation on the popular Western side dish can be used as an accompaniment to just about any main course dish, not just Indian food. There are easily obtainable alternatives to mango powder if you cannot get hold of any (see Cook's Tip).

15ml/1 tbsp chopped fresh mint and coriander (cilantro), mixed
5ml/1 tsp mango powder (amchur)
5ml/1 tsp salt
5ml/1 tsp crushed black peppercorns
1 fresh red chilli, chopped
1 fresh green chilli, chopped
50g/2oz/¼ cup butter

Serves 4

3 medium potatoes

1 Put the potatoes in a large pan. Add water to cover and bring to the boil. Add salt, then simmer for about 15 minutes, or until the potatoes are tender, but do not let them get too soft.

2 Drain thoroughly and leave to cool slightly, then mash them down using a masher or potato ricer.

3 Stir all the remaining ingredients together in a small mixing bowl until well combined.

4 Stir the spice mixture into the mashed potatoes. Mix together thoroughly with a fork and serve warm.

> **Cook's Tip**
> *Mango powder, also known as amchur, is the unripe green fruit of the mango tree ground to a powder. The sour mangoes are sliced and dried in the sun, turning a light brown, before they are ground. Mango powder adds a fruity sharpness and a slightly resinous bouquet to a dish. It is widely used with vegetables and is usually added towards the end of the cooking time. If mango powder is unavailable, the nearest substitute is lemon or lime juice, in double or treble quantity.*

Potato and Endive Mash

This unusual and very nutritious variant of mashed potato is made with raw endive and flavoured with the mild smoky taste Gouda cheese.

Serves 4

1kg/2¼lb potatoes, peeled and cut into even chunks

200g/7oz/1¾ cups diced mild Gouda cheese
1kg/2¼lb frisée lettuce, cut into thin strips
25g/1oz/2 tbsp butter
100ml/3½ fl oz/scant ½ cup milk
salt
butter or gravy, to serve

1 Cook the potatoes in lightly salted boiling water for about 20 minutes, until tender.

2 Drain the potatoes, return to the pan and mash with the butter and enough of the milk to make a smooth but not thin purée.

3 Stir in the frisée lettuce and diced cheese and cook in the microwave for ten seconds, until the cheese has started to melt.

4 Serve the potatoes immediately. This is delicious when eaten with a well in the centre for a knob (pat) of butter or a spoonful of gravy.

> **Cook's Tip**
> *Firm-textured potatoes such as Desirée, Pentland Dell and Estima are perfect for this dish. If you can't locate Gouda cheese, look out for a medium Cheddar or use Monterey Jack.*

> **Variation**
> *As an alternative to endive, turnip tops (greens), nettles, spinach, purslane, watercress or rocket (arugula) can also be served in this way.*

Endive Mash Energy 368kcal/1543kJ; Protein 14.6g; Carbohydrate 48.5g, of which sugars 6.2g; Fat 16g, of which saturates 7.4g; Cholesterol 41.2mg; Calcium 101.2mg; Fibre 4.7g; Sodium 848.7mg.
Masala Mashed Potatoes Energy 219kcal/919kJ; Protein 3.1g; Carbohydrate 28.9g, of which sugars 3g; Fat 10.9g, of which saturates 6.7g; Cholesterol 27mg; Calcium 13mg; Fibre 1.8g; Sodium 600mg.

Yorkshire Potato Puffs

Mini Yorkshire puddings with a soft centre of herby potato mash will be delicious with Sunday lunch, or serve them for supper with vegetarian sausages.

Makes 6
275g/10oz floury potatoes
creamy milk and butter,
  for mashing
5ml/1 tsp chopped fresh parsley
5ml/1 tsp chopped fresh tarragon
75g/3oz/⅔ cup plain
  (all-purpose) flour
1 egg
120ml/4fl oz/½ cup milk
vegetable oil or sunflower fat,
  for baking
salt and ground black pepper

1 Cook the potatoes in a large pan of boiling water until tender, then mash with a little creamy milk and butter. Stir in the chopped parsley and tarragon and season well to taste. Preheat the oven to 200°C/400°F/Gas 6.

2 Process the flour, egg, milk and a little salt in a food processor fitted with the metal blade, or a blender, to make a smooth batter.

3 Place about 2.5ml/½ tsp of oil or a small knob (pat) of sunflower fat in each of six ramekin dishes and place in the oven on a baking tray for 2–3 minutes until the oil or fat is very hot.

4 Working quickly, pour a small amount of batter (about 20ml/4 tsp) into each ramekin dish. Add a heaped tablespoon of the mashed potatoes and then pour an equal amount of the remaining batter in each dish. Bake for around 15–20 minutes until the puddings are puffy and golden brown.

5 Using a metal spatula, ease the puddings out of the ramekin dishes and arrange on a large serving dish. Serve immediately.

> **Cook's Tip**
> Cook and mash the potatoes the day before to save time, making a quick supper dish, or to prepare for a dinner party in advance.

Sautéed Potatoes with Rosemary

These rosemary-scented, crisp golden potatoes are a firm favourite in many households. They make a great alternative to chips or roast potatoes to partner grilled or roasted vegetables.

Serves 6
1.5kg/3lb firm baking potatoes
60–90ml/4–6 tbsp oil or
  clarified butter
2 fresh rosemary sprigs,
  leaves chopped
salt and ground black pepper

1 Using a vegetable peeler or sharp knife, peel the potatoes and then cut into 2.5cm/1in slices.

2 Place the slices in a bowl of cold water and soak for 10 minutes. Drain, rinse and then drain thoroughly. Pat dry with kitchen paper.

3 In a large frying pan, heat 60ml/4 tbsp of the oil, dripping or butter over a medium-high heat until hot, but not smoking. Add the potatoes to the pan and cook for 2 minutes without stirring so that they seal completely and brown on one side.

4 Shake the pan and toss the potatoes to brown on another side. Continue to shake the pan until the potatoes are browned on all sides. Season with plenty of salt and ground black pepper.

5 Add a little more oil, dripping or butter to the frying pan, reduce the heat to medium-low to low, and continue cooking the potatoes for about 20–25 minutes until tender, stirring and shaking the pan frequently. Test them by piercing with the tip of a knife or metal skewer.

6 About 5 minutes before the end of the cooking time, generously sprinkle the potatoes with chopped fresh rosemary. Serve immediately.

> **Cook's Tip**
> Try to cut the slices of potato as uniformly as possible: this will ensure that the slices are evenly cooked and beautifully golden.

Potato Puffs Energy 146kcal/614kJ; Protein 3.7g; Carbohydrate 18.1g, of which sugars 1.8g; Fat 7.1g, of which saturates 1.1g; Cholesterol 33mg; Calcium 52mg; Fibre 0.9g; Sodium 29mg.
Sautéed Potatoes Energy 264kcal/1108kJ; Protein 4.1g; Carbohydrate 38.5g, of which sugars 3.7g; Fat 11.4g, of which saturates 1.5g; Cholesterol 0mg; Calcium 17mg; Fibre 2.5g; Sodium 26mg.

Potatoes with Roasted Poppy Seeds

Poppy seeds are used in Indian cooking as thickening agents, and to lend a nutty taste to sauces.

Serves 4

45ml/3 tbsp white poppy seeds
45–60ml/3–4 tbsp vegetable oil
675g/1½lb potatoes, peeled and cut into 1cm/½in cubes
2.5ml/½ tsp black mustard seeds
2.5ml/½ tsp onion seeds
2.5ml/½ tsp cumin seeds
2.5ml/½ tsp fennel seeds
1 or 2 dried red chillies, chopped or broken into small pieces
2.5ml/½ tsp ground turmeric
2.5ml/½ tsp salt
150ml/¼ pint/⅔ cup warm water
fresh coriander (cilantro) sprigs, to garnish
pooris and natural (plain) yogurt, to serve

1 Preheat a karahi, wok or large pan over a medium setting. When the pan is hot, reduce the heat slightly and add the poppy seeds. Stir them around in the pan until they are just a shade darker. Remove from the pan and leave to cool.

2 In the pan, heat the vegetable oil over a medium heat and fry the cubes of potato until they are light brown. Remove them with a slotted spoon and drain on kitchen paper.

3 To the same oil, add the mustard seeds. As soon as they begin to pop, add the onion, cumin and fennel seeds and the chillies. Let the chillies blacken, but remove them from the pan before they burn.

4 Stir in the turmeric and follow quickly with the fried potatoes and salt. Stir well and add the warm water. Cover the pan with the lid and reduce the heat to low. Cook for 8–10 minutes, or until the potatoes are tender.

5 Grind the poppy seeds in a mortar and pestle or spice grinder. Stir the ground seeds into the potatoes. This should form a thick paste which should cling firmly to the potatoes. If there is too much liquid, continue to stir over a medium heat until you have the right consistency. Transfer to a serving dish. Garnish with coriander and serve with pooris and natural yogurt.

Berrichonne Potatoes

A potato dish with a difference. The top of the potatoes will be crispy with a soft base cooked in the stock, onions and butter.

1 onion, finely chopped
350ml/12fl oz /1½ cups vegetable stock
chopped fresh parsley, to garnish
sea salt and ground black pepper

Serves 4

900g/2lb maincrop potatoes
25g/1oz/2 tbsp butter

1 Preheat the oven to 200°C/400°F/Gas 6. Peel the potatoes and trim them into barrel shapes. Leave the potatoes to stand in a bowl of cold water.

2 Melt the butter in a heavy frying pan. Add the chopped onions, stir to coat in the butter and cover the pan with a tight-fitting lid. Cook gently for 5–7 minutes, until they have softened but not turned brown.

3 Spoon the onion mixture into the base of a 1.5 litre/ 2½ pint/6¼ cup rectangular shallow ovenproof dish.

4 Lay the potatoes over the onion mixture and pour the stock over, making sure that it comes halfway up the sides.

5 Season with salt and pepper and bake in the preheated oven for about 1 hour until crisp and beautifully golden brown on top. Garnish with chopped parsley and serve.

Variations
• Crumble over some deliciously salty feta cheese for the last 10 minutes of cooking time.
• Add some whole, unpeeled garlic cloves to the dish before putting it in the oven. After cooking the garlic will be deliciously soft and sweet, and can be easily squeezed out its skin.
• Other vegetables can be cooked in this way, try a mixture of root vegetables; such as parsnips, celeriac and turnips.

Potatoes with Seeds Energy 260kcal/1091kJ; Protein 6.2g; Carbohydrate 30.2g, of which sugars 4.7g; Fat 6.9g, of which saturates 0.9g; Cholesterol 0mg; Calcium 205mg; Fibre 4.3g; Sodium 668mg.
Berrichonne Potatoes Energy 289kcal/1213kJ; Protein 8.6g; Carbohydrate 37.5g, of which sugars 3.8g; Fat 12.6g, of which saturates 5.9g; Cholesterol 32mg; Calcium 20mg; Fibre 2.5g; Sodium 425mg.

Deep-fried New Potatoes with Saffron Aioli

Serve these crispy little golden potatoes dipped into a wickedly garlicky mayonnaise – then watch them disappear in a matter of minutes. They make an ideal accompaniment to most dishes or are equally tasty as a snack.

Serves 4

1 egg yolk
2.5ml/½ tsp Dijon mustard
300ml/½ pint/1¼ cups extra
   virgin olive oil
15–30ml/1–2 tbsp lemon juice
1 garlic clove, crushed
2.5ml/½ tsp saffron strands
20 baby, new or salad potatoes
vegetable oil, for deep frying
salt and ground black pepper

1 For the aioli, put the egg yolk in a small mixing bowl with the mustard and a pinch of salt. Mix until combined. Beat in the olive oil very slowly, drop by drop, then in a thin stream. Add the lemon juice.

2 Season the aioli with salt and ground black pepper, then add the crushed garlic and beat the mixture thoroughly until well combined.

3 Place the saffron in a small bowl and add 10ml/2 tsp of hot water. Press the saffron firmly, using the back of a teaspoon, to extract the colour and flavour, and leave to infuse (steep) for around 5 minutes. Beat the saffron and the infused liquid into the aioli.

4 Cook the potatoes in their skins in boiling salted water for 5 minutes, then turn off the heat. Cover the pan and leave for about 15 minutes. Drain the potatoes, then dry them thoroughly in a clean dish towel.

5 Heat a 1cm/½in layer of vegetable oil in a deep pan. When the oil is very hot, add the potatoes and fry them quickly, turning them occasionally until they are crisp and golden brown all over. Drain them thoroughly on kitchen paper and serve hot with the saffron aioli.

Potatoes, Peppers and Shallots Roasted with Rosemary

These potatoes soak up both the taste and wonderful aromas of the shallots and the fresh rosemary sprigs. Serve this as an accompaniment to a vegetarian barbecue.

12 shallots
2 sweet yellow (bell) peppers
olive oil
2 rosemary sprigs
salt and ground black pepper
olive oil
crushed peppercorns, to garnish

Serves 4

500g/1¼lb waxy potatoes

1 Preheat the oven to 200°C/400°F/Gas 6. Par-boil the potatoes in their skins in boiling salted water for 5 minutes. Drain, and when they are cool, peel them and halve lengthways.

2 Peel the shallots, allowing them to fall into their natural segments. Cut each sweet pepper lengthways into eight strips, discarding seeds and pith.

3 Oil a shallow ovenproof dish thoroughly with olive oil. Arrange the potatoes and peppers in alternating rows and stud with the shallots.

4 Cut the rosemary sprigs into 5cm/2in lengths and tuck among the vegetables. Season the vegetables generously with salt and pepper, then toss in the olive oil.

5 Roast, uncovered, in the oven for 30–40 minutes until all the vegetables are tender. Turn the vegetables occasionally to cook and brown evenly. Serve hot or at room temperature, with crushed peppercorns.

Cook's Tip
Liven up a simple midweek supper with these delicious and easy potatoes.

Deep-fried Potatoes Energy 795kcal/3282kJ; Protein 2.9g; Carbohydrate 20.1g, of which sugars 1.6g; Fat 78.7g, of which saturates 10.5g; Cholesterol 50mg; Calcium 13mg; Fibre 1.3g; Sodium 16mg.
Potatoes with Rosemary Energy 176kcal/742kJ; Protein 4.2g; Carbohydrate 33.6g, of which sugars 12.6g; Fat 3.7g, of which saturates 0.6g; Cholesterol 0mg; Calcium 40mg; Fibre 4.1g; Sodium 20mg.

Roasted Root Vegetables with Whole Spice Seeds

These fragrantly spiced vegetables are the perfect accompaniment to a spicy main course. They will virtually look after themselves and make a delicious side dish.

Serves 4
3 parsnips, peeled
3 potatoes, peeled
3 carrots, peeled
3 sweet potatoes, peeled
60ml/4 tbsp olive oil
8 shallots, peeled
2 garlic cloves, sliced
10ml/2 tsp white mustard seeds
10ml/2 tsp coriander seeds, lightly crushed
5ml/1 tsp cumin seeds
2 bay leaves
salt and ground black pepper

1 Preheat the oven to 190°C/375°F/Gas 5. Bring a pan of lightly salted water to the boil. Cut the parsnips, potatoes, carrots and sweet potatoes into chunks. Add them to the pan and bring the water back to the boil. Boil for 2 minutes, then drain the vegetables thoroughly.

2 Pour the olive oil into a large, heavy roasting pan and place over a moderate heat. When the oil is hot, add the drained vegetables, together with the whole shallots and garlic. Fry, tossing the vegetables over the heat, until they are pale golden at the edges.

3 Add the mustard, coriander and cumin seeds and the bay leaves. Cook for 1 minute, then season with salt and pepper.

4 Transfer the roasting pan to the oven and roast for about 45 minutes, turning the vegetables occasionally, until they are crisp and golden and cooked through.

Variation
Vary the selection of vegetables according to what is available. Try using swede (rutabaga) or pumpkin instead of, or as well as, the vegetables suggested.

Roasted Potatoes with Red Onions

These mouthwatering potatoes are a great accompaniment to just about anything. The key is to use small firm potatoes; the smaller they are cut, the less time they will take to cook.

Serves 4
675 g/1½lb small firm potatoes
25 g/1oz/2 tbsp butter
30ml/2 tbsp olive oil
2 red onions, cut into chunks
8 garlic cloves, unpeeled
30ml/2 tbsp chopped fresh rosemary
salt and ground black pepper

1 Preheat the oven to 230°C/450°F/Gas 8. Peel and quarter the potatoes, rinse them well and pat thoroughly dry on kitchen paper.

2 Place the butter and olive oil in a roasting pan and place in the oven to heat.

3 When the butter has melted and is foaming, add the potatoes, red onions, garlic and rosemary. Toss well, then spread out in one layer.

4 Place the pan in the oven and roast for about 25 minutes until the potatoes are golden and tender when tested with a fork. Shake the pan from time to time whilst cooking to redistribute the potatoes. When cooked, season with salt and ground black pepper before serving.

Cook's Tip
To ensure that the potatoes are crisp, make sure they are completely dry before cooking. Resist the urge to turn the potatoes too often. Allow them to brown on one side before turning. Do not salt the potatoes until the end of cooking – salting beforehand encourages them to give up their liquid, making them limp.

Root Vegetables Energy 290kcal/1213kJ; Protein 11.5g; Carbohydrate 32.5g, of which sugars 13.3g; Fat 13.6g, of which saturates 1.6g; Cholesterol 0mg; Calcium 175mg; Fibre 9.1g; Sodium 271mg.
Roasted Potatoes Energy 254kcal/1063kJ; Protein 4.5g; Carbohydrate 35.4g, of which sugars 8.1g; Fat 11.5g, of which saturates 4.2g; Cholesterol 13mg; Calcium 59mg; Fibre 3.7g; Sodium 63mg.

Baked Anglesey Eggs and Potatoes

This creamy dish of
potatoes, leeks, eggs and
cheese sauce makes a
perfect warming winter
lunch and is equally
delicious when served as
part of an evening meal.

Serves 4
500g/1lb 2oz potatoes, peeled

3 leeks, sliced
6 eggs
600ml/1 pint/2½ cups milk
50g/2oz/½ cup plain
  (all-purpose) flour
100g/3½oz/1 cup Caerphilly
  cheese, grated
25g/1oz fresh root ginger, peeled
  and grated
salt and ground black pepper

1 Cook the potatoes in boiling water for about 15 minutes or
until soft. Meanwhile, cook the leeks in a little water for about
10 minutes until soft. Hard-boil the eggs, drain and put under
cold running water to cool them.

2 Preheat the oven to 200°C/400°F/Gas 6. Drain and mash
the potatoes.

3 Drain the leeks and stir into the potatoes with a little black
pepper. Remove the shells from the eggs and cut into quarters.

4 Pour the milk into a pan and add the butter and flour.
Stirring constantly with a whisk, bring slowly to the boil
and bubble gently for 2 minutes, until thickened, smooth and
glossy. Remove from the heat, stir in half of the Caerphilly
cheese and season to taste.

5 Arrange the eggs in four shallow ovenproof dishes. Spoon the
potato and leek mixture into the dishes. Pour the cheese sauce
over the top with the remaining cheese. Put into the hot oven
and cook for 15–20 minutes, until bubbling and golden brown.
Serve immediately.

> **Cook's Tip**
> The leeks could be cooked in the microwave in a covered dish:
> there is no need to add water. Stir once or twice during cooking.

Potato-stuffed Aubergines

This typical Ligurian dish is
spiked with paprika and
allspice, a legacy from the
days when spices imported
from the East came into
northern Italy via the port
of Genoa.

Serves 4
2 aubergines, about 225g/8oz
  each, stalks removed
275g/10oz potatoes, peeled
  and diced

30ml/2 tbsp olive oil
1 small onion, finely chopped
1 garlic clove, finely chopped
good pinch of ground allspice
  and paprika
1 egg, beaten
40g/1½oz/½ cup grated
  Parmesan cheese
15ml/1 tbsp fresh
  white breadcrumbs
salt and ground black pepper
fresh mint sprigs, to garnish
salad leaves, to serve

1 Bring a large pan of lightly salted water to the boil. Add the
whole aubergines and cook for 5 minutes, turning frequently.
Remove with a slotted spoon and set aside. Add the potatoes
to the pan and cook for 20 minutes until soft.

2 Meanwhile, cut the aubergines in half lengthways and gently
scoop out the flesh with a small sharp knife and a spoon,
leaving 5mm/¼in of the shell intact. Select a baking dish that will
hold the aubergines snugly in a single layer. Brush it lightly with
oil. Put the shells in the baking dish and chop the aubergine
flesh roughly.

3 Heat the oil in a frying pan, add the onion and cook gently,
stirring frequently, until softened. Add the chopped aubergine
flesh and the garlic. Cook, stirring frequently, for 6–8 minutes.
Tip into a bowl. Preheat the oven to 190°C/375°F/Gas 5.

4 Drain and mash the potatoes. Add to the aubergine mixture
with the spices and egg. Set aside 15ml/1 tbsp of the Parmesan
and add the rest to the aubergine mixture. Season to taste.

5 Spoon the mixture into the aubergine shells. Mix together the
breadcrumbs with the reserved Parmesan cheese and sprinkle
the mixture over the aubergines. Bake for around 40–45 minutes
until the topping is crisp. Garnish with mint and serve with salad.

Stuffed Aubergines Energy 193kcal/809kJ; Protein 8g; Carbohydrate 17.6g, of which sugars 4.1g; Fat 10.6g, of which saturates 3.3g; Cholesterol 48mg; Calcium 150mg; Fibre 3.2g; Sodium 162mg.
Anglesey Eggs Energy 540kcal/2259kJ; Protein 26.6g; Carbohydrate 41.3g, of which sugars 12.3g; Fat 30.6g, of which saturates 16.2g; Cholesterol 345mg; Calcium 471mg; Fibre 5g; Sodium 443mg.

Potato and Pumpkin Pudding

Serve this savoury pumpkin and potato pudding with a rich autumnal casserole or simply with a mixed salad.

Serves 4
45ml/3 tbsp olive oil
1 garlic clove, sliced
675g/1½lb pumpkin flesh, cut into 2cm/¾ in chunks

350g/12oz potatoes
25g/1oz/2 tbsp butter
90g/3½oz/scant ½ cup ricotta cheese
50g/2oz/⅔ cup grated Parmesan cheese
pinch grated nutmeg
4 eggs, separated
salt and ground black pepper
chopped fresh parsley, to garnish

1 Preheat the oven to 200°C/400°F/Gas 6. Grease a 1.75 litre/ 3 pint/7½ cup shallow, oval baking dish.

2 Heat the oil in a large shallow pan, add the garlic and pumpkin and cook, stirring often to prevent sticking, for 15–20 minutes or until the pumpkin is tender.

3 Meanwhile, cook the potatoes in boiling salted water for 20 minutes until tender. Drain, leave until cool enough to handle, then peel off the skins. Place the potatoes and pumpkin in a large bowl and mash well with the butter.

4 Mash the ricotta with a fork until smooth and add to the potato and pumpkin mixture, mixing well. Stir the Parmesan, nutmeg and seasoning into the mixture – it should be smooth and creamy. Mix in the egg yolks one at a time.

5 Whisk the egg whites with an electric whisk until they form stiff peaks, then fold gently into the mixture. Spoon into the prepared baking dish and bake for 30 minutes until golden and firm. Serve hot, garnished with parsley.

> **Cook's Tip**
> *You may process the vegetables in a food processor for a few seconds, but be careful not to overprocess, as they will become very gluey.*

Boulangère Potatoes

This tasty dish features layers of potato and onions cooked in butter and stock. This is a delicious savoury potato dish that makes a great accompaniment to a hearty winter casserole.

Serves 6
butter for greasing

450g/1lb maincrop potatoes, very finely sliced
2 onions, finely sliced into rings
2 garlic cloves, crushed
50g/2oz/¼ cup butter, diced
300ml/½ pint/1¼ cups vegetable stock
chopped parsley
sea salt and ground black pepper

1 Preheat the oven to 180°C/350°F/Gas 4. Grease the base and sides of a 1.5 litre/2½ pint/6¼ cup shallow ovenproof dish.

2 Line the dish with some of the sliced potatoes. Sprinkle some onions and garlic on top. Layer up the remaining potatoes and onions. Season between each layer with salt and black pepper.

3 Push the vegetables down into the dish and dot the top with the butter. Pour the stock over and bake in the preheated oven for about 1½ hours

4 After 1 hour, if the top starts to brown too much, then cover with a piece of foil. Serve with parsley and plenty of salt and pepper sprinkled over the top.

> **Cook's Tip**
> *Slice the potatoes for this dish as thin as you can. A mandolin is an ideal kitchen tool for this job, although be careful when using as they have very sharp blades.*

> **Variation**
> *If you want to make this dish more substantial, add some grated cheese, sprinkled over the top just before you bake it.*

Potato Pudding Energy 434kcal/1801kJ; Protein 14.7g; Carbohydrate 18g, of which sugars 4g; Fat 34.3g, of which saturates 15.6g; Cholesterol 239mg; Calcium 256mg; Fibre 2.6g; Sodium 330mg.
Boulangère Potatoes Energy 118kcal/494kJ; Protein 1.5g; Carbohydrate 12.9g, of which sugars 1.6g; Fat 7.1g, of which saturates 4.4g; Cholesterol 18mg; Calcium 9mg; Fibre 0.9g; Sodium 59mg.

Potato Pan Gratin

Potatoes, layered with mustard butter and baked until golden, are perfect to serve with a green salad for supper, or as an accompaniment to a vegetable or nut roast.

Serves 4

4 large potatoes, total weight about 900g/2lb

25g/1oz/2 tbsp butter
15ml/1 tbsp olive oil
2 large garlic cloves, crushed
30ml/2 tbsp Dijon mustard
15ml/1 tbsp lemon juice
15ml/1 tbsp fresh thyme leaves, plus extra to garnish
50ml/2fl oz/¼ cup vegetable stock
salt and ground black pepper

1 Thinly slice the potatoes using a knife or a slicing attachment on a food processor. Place in a bowl of cold water to prevent them discolouring.

2 Preheat the oven to 200°C/400°F/Gas 6. Heat the butter and oil in a deep, flameproof frying pan. Add the garlic and cook gently for 3 minutes until light golden, stirring constantly. Stir in the mustard, lemon juice and thyme. Remove from the heat and pour the mixture into a jug (pitcher).

3 Drain the potatoes and pat dry with kitchen paper. Place a layer of potatoes in the frying pan, season and pour over one-third of the butter mixture. Place another layer of potatoes on top, season, and pour over another third of the butter mixture. Arrange a final layer of potatoes on top, pour over the rest of the butter mixture and then the stock. Season and sprinkle with the reserved thyme.

4 Cover the top with baking parchment and bake for 1 hour, then remove the paper and cook for a further 15 minutes or until golden. Serve immediately.

Variation
Any root vegetables can be used in this dish: try celeriac, parsnips, swede (rutabaga) or turnips.

Potatoes Baked with Fennel, Onions, Garlic and Saffron

Potatoes, fennel and onions infused with garlic, saffron and fragrant spices make a sophisticated, attractive and delicious accompaniment for an egg-based main course dish.

Serves 4–6

500g/1¼lb small waxy potatoes, cut into chunks or wedges
good pinch of saffron strands (12–15 strands)
1 head of garlic, separated into cloves

12 small red or yellow onions, peeled but left whole
3 fennel bulbs, cut into wedges, feathery tops reserved
4–6 fresh bay leaves
6–9 fresh thyme sprigs
175ml/6fl oz/¾ cup vegetable stock
30ml/2 tbsp sherry vinegar
2.5ml/½ tsp sugar
5ml/1 tsp fennel seeds, lightly crushed
2.5ml/½ tsp paprika
45ml/3 tbsp olive oil
salt and ground black pepper

1 Put the potatoes in a large pan. Add water to cover and bring to the boil. Add salt, then simmer for about 8–10 minutes, or until the potatoes are just tender. Drain thoroughly.

2 Preheat the oven to 190°C/375°F/Gas 5. Place the saffron strands in a bowl with 30ml/2 tbsp warm water and leave to infuse (steep) for 10 minutes.

3 Peel and finely chop two garlic cloves. Place the potatoes, onions, the remaining unpeeled garlic cloves, fennel wedges, bay leaves and thyme sprigs in a roasting pan.

4 Mix together the stock, saffron and its soaking liquid, vinegar and sugar, then pour over the vegetables. Stir in the fennel seeds, paprika, chopped garlic and olive oil, and season with salt and pepper.

5 Place the pan in the oven and bake for 1–1¼ hours, stirring occasionally, until the vegetables are tender. Chop the reserved feathery tops of the fennel, sprinkle over the vegetables and serve immediately.

Potato Pan Gratin Energy 238kcal/1002kJ; Protein 3.9g; Carbohydrate 36.3g, of which sugars 3g; Fat 9.6g, of which saturates 4.5g; Cholesterol 16mg; Calcium 15mg; Fibre 2.3g; Sodium 70mg.
Potatoes Baked with Fennel Energy 162kcal/676kJ; Protein 4.4g; Carbohydrate 23.6g, of which sugars 7.1g; Fat 6.2g, of which saturates 0.9g; Cholesterol 0mg; Calcium 49mg; Fibre 4.9g; Sodium 23mg.

Herby Potato Bake

This dish features wonderfully creamy potatoes that are well flavoured with lots of fresh herbs, and sprinkled with cheese to make a golden, crunchy topping. Serve as an accompaniment to grilled vegetable skewers.

Serves 4

butter, for greasing
675g/1½lb waxy potatoes

25g/1oz/2 tbsp butter
1 onion, finely chopped
1 garlic clove, crushed
2 eggs
300ml/½ pint/1¼ cups crème
   fraîche or double (heavy) cream
115g/4oz/1 cup Gruyère
   cheese, grated
60ml/4 tbsp chopped mixed fresh
   herbs, such as chervil, thyme,
   chives and parsley
freshly grated nutmeg
salt and ground black pepper

1 Place a baking sheet in the oven and preheat to 190°C/375°F/Gas 5. Butter an ovenproof dish.

2 Peel the potatoes and cut them into matchsticks. Set aside while you make up the sauce mixture.

3 Start by melting the butter in a heavy pan and cook the onion and garlic for 5–7 minutes until softened. Remove from the heat to cool slightly.

4 In a large mixing bowl, whisk together the eggs, crème fraîche or double cream and about half of the grated Gruyère cheese. Whisk thoroughly until all the ingredients are well combined.

5 Stir the onion mixture, mixed herbs and potatoes into the creamy egg mixture. Season with plenty of salt and ground black pepper, and sprinkle with the grated nutmeg. Spoon the mixture into the prepared dish and top with a sprinkling of the remaining cheese.

6 Place the dish in the oven on the hot baking sheet and bake for 50 minutes to 1 hour until the top is golden brown and the potato is tender. Serve immediately, straight from the dish, as this will ensure that the potatoes stay really hot.

Potatoes and Parsnips with Garlic and Cream

For the best results, cut the potatoes and parsnips very thinly – use a mandolin if you have one. As an alternative this method is also ideal for cooking sweet potatoes, which will produce a sweeter candied, but equally delicious, result.

Serves 4–6

3 large potatoes, total weight
   about 675g/1½lb
2 garlic cloves, crushed

350g/12oz small to
   medium parsnips
200ml/7fl oz/scant 1 cup single
   (light) cream
100ml/3½fl oz/scant ½ cup milk
butter, for greasing
about 5ml/1 tsp freshly
   grated nutmeg
75g/3oz/¾ cup coarsely
   grated Cheddar or Red
   Leicester cheese
salt and ground black pepper

1 Peel the potatoes and parsnips and cut them into thin slices. Cook in a large pan of salted boiling water for around 5 minutes. Drain and cool slightly.

2 Meanwhile, pour the cream and milk into a heavy pan and add the crushed garlic. Bring to the boil over a medium heat, then remove from the heat and leave to stand for about 10 minutes.

3 Preheat the oven to 180°C/350°F/Gas 4 and lightly butter the bottom and sides of a shallow ovenproof dish. Arrange the potatoes and parsnips in the dish, sprinkling each layer with a little freshly grated nutmeg, salt and ground black pepper.

4 Pour the liquid into the dish and press the potatoes and parsnips down into it. Cover with lightly buttered foil and cook in the hot oven for 45 minutes.

5 Remove the foil and sprinkle the cheese over the vegetables. Return the dish to the oven and continue cooking, uncovered, for a further 20–30 minutes, or until the potatoes and parsnips are tender and the top is golden brown.

Herby Potato Bake Energy 614kcal/2550kJ; Protein 15.6g; Carbohydrate 30.6g, of which sugars 5g; Fat 48g, of which saturates 30.8g; Cholesterol 221mg; Calcium 310mg; Fibre 2.5g; Sodium 321mg.
Potatoes and Parsnips Energy 241kcal/1012kJ; Protein 7.8g; Carbohydrate 27.2g, of which sugars 6.4g; Fat 11.7g, of which saturates 7.2g; Cholesterol 31mg; Calcium 173mg; Fibre 3.9g; Sodium 126mg.

Potato, Onion and Garlic Gratin

This is a simple but delicious way of cooking potatoes and onions together. When cooked the top layer of potatoes is deliciously crispy and gives way to a soft and sumptuous filling that is infused with a moreish garlicky kick. The perfect side dish for any vegetarian feast.

Serves 4–6
40g/1½oz/3 tbsp butter or
*   45ml/3 tbsp olive oil*
2–4 garlic cloves, finely chopped
900g/2lb waxy potatoes,
*   thinly sliced*
450g/1lb onions, thinly sliced
450ml/¾ pint/scant 2 cups
*   vegetable stock*
salt and ground black pepper

1 Use half the butter or oil to grease a 1.5 litre/2½ pint/ 6¼ cup gratin dish. Preheat the oven to 180°C/350°F/Gas 4.

2 Sprinkle a little of the chopped garlic over the base of the dish and then layer the potatoes and onions in the dish, seasoning each layer with a little salt and pepper and adding the remaining garlic. Finish with a layer of overlapping potato slices on top.

3 Bring the stock to the boil in a pan and pour it over the gratin. Dot the top with the remaining butter, or drizzle over the reserved oil. Cover tightly with foil and bake for 1½ hours.

4 Increase the oven temperature to 200°C/400°F/Gas 6. Uncover the gratin and then cook for a further 35–50 minutes, until the potatoes are completely cooked and the top layer is browned and crusty. Serve immediately.

Variation
Layer 175g/6oz thinly sliced cheese with the potatoes. About 15–20 minutes before the end of cooking time, sprinkle the gratin with another 50g/2oz/½ cup grated cheese, dot with more butter and finish baking. This version is also good made with leeks.

Colcannon

This traditional Irish potato dish is especially associated with Halloween, when it is likely to be made with curly kale and would have a ring hidden in it - predicting marriage during the coming year for the person who found it. However, it is also served throughout the winter, when green cabbage is more often used.

Serves 3–4 as a main dish, or 6–8 as a side dish
450g/1lb potatoes, peeled
*   and boiled*
450g/1lb curly kale or
*   cabbage, cooked*
milk, if necessary
50g/2oz/2 tbsp butter, plus extra
*   for serving*
1 large onion,
*   finely chopped*
salt and ground black pepper

1 Mash the potatoes. Chop the curly kale or cabbage, add it to the potatoes and mix to combine. Stir in a little milk if the mash is too stiff.

2 Melt a little butter in a frying pan over a medium heat and add the onion, Cook until softened, but not browned. Remove from the heat and mix well with the mashed potato and kale or cabbage mixture.

3 Add the remainder of the butter to the hot pan. When very hot, turn the potato mixture on to the pan and spread it out. Fry until golden brown and crispy.

4 Cut the colcannon into roughly sized pieces and continue frying until they are crisp and brown on all sides, taking care not to burn.

5 Serve in warmed bowls, or as a side dish to roasted or braised meats with plenty of butter.

Variation
Try varying the dish, by adding cooked swede (rutabaga) or turnip before mashing, or mixing in some freshly chopped mixed herbs with the kale or cabbage.

Potato Gratin Energy 181kcal/762kJ; Protein 3.5g; Carbohydrate 30.1g, of which sugars 6.2g; Fat 6.1g, of which saturates 3.8g; Cholesterol 15mg; Calcium 29mg; Fibre 2.6g; Sodium 69mg.
Colcannon Energy 306kcal/1281kJ; Protein 5.4g; Carbohydrate 40.6g, of which sugars 13.6g; Fat 14.6g, of which saturates 8.8g; Cholesterol 36mg; Calcium 104mg; Fibre 5.9g; Sodium 127mg.

Potato and Spinach Gratin

Pine nuts add a satisfying crunch to this gratin of wafer-thin potato slices and spinach in a wonderfully creamy cheese sauce.

Serves 2

450g/1lb potatoes
1 garlic clove, crushed
3 spring onions (scallions), thinly sliced
150ml/¼ pint/⅔ cup single (light) cream
250ml/8fl oz/1 cup milk
225g/8oz frozen chopped spinach, thawed
115g/4oz/1 cup grated mature (sharp) Cheddar cheese
25g/1oz/¼ cup pine nuts
salt and ground black pepper
lettuce and tomato salad, to serve

1 Peel the potatoes and cut them carefully into wafer-thin slices. This is most easily done with a mandoline or the slicing attachment of a food processor. Spread the slices out in a large, heavy, non-stick frying pan.

2 Sprinkle the crushed garlic and sliced spring onions evenly over the potatoes.

3 Mix together the cream and milk in a jug (pitcher) and pour the mixture over the potatoes. Place the pan over low heat, cover with a tight-fitting lid and cook for 8 minutes, or until the potatoes are tender.

4 Drain the spinach thoroughly, then, using both hands, squeeze it as dry as possible. Add the spinach to the potatoes, mixing lightly. Cover the pan with a tight-fitting lid and cook for 2 minutes more.

5 Season to taste with salt and pepper, then spoon the mixture into a gratin dish. Preheat the grill (broiler).

6 Sprinkle the grated cheese and pine nuts evenly over the potato and spinach mixture. Lightly toast under the grill for around 2–3 minutes, until the cheese has melted and the topping is bubbling and golden brown. Serve the gratin immediately as a side dish, or for a light meal with a lettuce and tomato salad.

Byron Potatoes

A meal in itself, this dish is based on baked potatoes with a creamy cheese filling.

Serves 6

3 baking potatoes
115g/4oz/1 cup mature (sharp) Cheddar cheese, grated
90ml/6 tbsp single (light) cream
sea salt and ground black pepper

1 Preheat the oven to 200°C/400°F/Gas 6. Scrub the potatoes and pat dry. Prick each one with a fork and cook directly on the middle shelf for 1 hour 20 minutes.

2 Remove the potatoes from the oven and halve. Place the halves on a baking sheet and make shallow dips in the centre of each potato, raising the potato up at the edges.

3 Mix the cheese and cream together and divide evenly between the potatoes. Grill (broil) for 5 minutes until the cheese has melted and started to bubble. Serve hot, sprinkled with salt and pepper.

Lacy Potato Pancakes

These pretty, lacy potato pancakes can be made as a side dish or scaled down and topped with sour cream and dill for an appetizer. Small pancakes make delicious canapés at parties.

Serves 6

6 large potatoes
1 leek, finely sliced
1 carrot, grated (optional)
15g/½oz/1 tbsp butter
15ml/1 tbsp vegetable oil
salt and ground black pepper

1 Peel and grate the potatoes. Put in a bowl, add the leek and carrot, if using, and mix them all together.

2 Heat the butter and oil in a frying pan and when smoking, add spoonfuls of the potato mixture to make 7.5cm/3in pancakes. Fry the pancakes, turning once, until golden brown on both sides. Season with salt and pepper and serve hot.

Potato Gratin Energy 248kcal/1037kJ; Protein 3.6g; Carbohydrate 30.7g, of which sugars 6.6g; Fat 13.2g, of which saturates 3.4g; Cholesterol 10mg; Calcium 31mg; Fibre 2.7g; Sodium 50mg.
Byron Potatoes Energy 180kcal/751kJ; Protein 7g; Carbohydrate 16.7g, of which sugars 1.9g; Fat 9.4g, of which saturates 6g; Cholesterol 27mg; Calcium 161mg; Fibre 1g; Sodium 157mg.
Lacy Pancakes Energy 182kcal/767kJ; Protein 3.9g; Carbohydrate 33.1g, of which sugars 3.3g; Fat 4.6g, of which saturates 1.8g; Cholesterol 5mg; Calcium 20mg; Fibre 2.7g; Sodium 38mg.

Potato Latkes

Latkes are traditional Jewish potato pancakes, fried until golden and crisp and sweet apple sauce and sour cream.

Serves 4
2 medium floury potatoes
1 onion
1 large egg, beaten
30ml/2 tbsp medium-ground matzo meal
vegetable oil, for frying
salt and ground black pepper
sour cream, to serve

1 Coarsely grate the potatoes and the onion. Put them in a large colander but don't rinse them. Press them down, squeezing out as much of the thick starchy liquid as possible. Transfer the potato mixture to a bowl.

2 Immediately stir the beaten egg into the potatoes. Add the matzo meal, stirring gently to mix. Season with salt and plenty of black pepper.

3 Heat a 1cm/½in layer of oil in a heavy frying pan for a few minutes (test it by throwing in a small piece of bread – it should sizzle). Take a spoonful of the potato mixture and lower it carefully into the oil. Continue adding spoonfuls, leaving space between each one.

4 Flatten the pancakes slightly with the back of a spoon. Fry for a few minutes until the latkes are golden brown on the underside, carefully turn them over and continue frying until golden brown.

5 Drain the latkes on kitchen paper, then transfer to an ovenproof serving dish and keep warm in a low oven while frying the remainder. Serve hot, topped with sour cream.

> **Variation**
> Try using equal quantities of potatoes and Jerusalem artichokes for a really distinct flavour.

Straw Potato Cake

This dish gets its name from its interesting straw-like appearance. Serve cut into wedges alongside roast vegetables as a change from the usual potato dishes.

Serves 4
450g/1lb firm baking potatoes
25ml/1½ tbsp butter, melted
15ml/1 tbsp vegetable oil
salt and ground black pepper

1 Peel and grate the potatoes, then toss with melted butter and season with salt and pepper.

2 Heat the oil in a large heavy frying pan. Add the potato and press down to form an even layer that covers the base of the pan. Cook over a medium heat for 7–10 minutes until the base is well browned.

3 Loosen the cake if it has stuck to the bottom by shaking the pan or running a knife under it. To turn the cake, invert a large baking tray over the frying pan and, holding it tightly against the pan, turn them both over together. Lift off the frying pan, return it to the heat and add a little more oil if it looks dry.

4 Slide the potato cake back into the frying pan, browned side uppermost, and continue cooking until the underside is crisp and golden. Serve the cake hot, cut into individual wedges.

> **Cook's Tip**
> Use the bigger side of a manual grater or a large blade on the food processor for the potatoes. They will then hold their shape better while being cooked than if you grate them finely.

> **Variation**
> Another nice way to serve this dish is to make several small cakes instead of a large one. They will not take quite so long to cook, so follow the method as for the large cake, but adjust the cooking time accordingly.

Potato Latkes Energy 221kcal/929kJ; Protein 4.3g; Carbohydrate 37.6g, of which sugars 20g; Fat 6.8g, of which saturates 1g; Cholesterol 43mg; Calcium 33mg; Fibre 2.7g; Sodium 28mg.
Straw Potato Cake Energy 146kcal/610kJ; Protein 2g; Carbohydrate 18.2g, of which sugars 1.5g; Fat 7.7g, of which saturates 3.4g; Cholesterol 12mg; Calcium 8mg; Fibre 1.1g; Sodium 47mg.

Cheese Bubble and Squeak

This London potato breakfast dish was originally made on Mondays with leftover vegetables from the previous Sunday's lunch.

Serves 4
about 450g/1lb/3 cups
   mashed potatoes
about 225g/8oz/4 cups shredded
   cooked cabbage or kale
1 egg, lightly beaten
115g/4oz/1 cup grated
   Cheddar cheese
pinch of freshly grated nutmeg
salt and ground black pepper
plain (all-purpose) flour,
   for coating
vegetable oil, for frying

1 Mix together the mashed potatoes, cabbage or kale, egg, cheese and nutmeg in a bowl and season with salt and pepper. Divide the mixture into eight pieces and shape into patties.

2 Place the patties on a large plate, cover with clear film (plastic wrap) and chill in the refrigerator for 1 hour or more, if possible, as this helps firm up the mixture.

3 Gently toss the patties in the flour to coat lightly. Heat about 1cm/½in oil in a frying pan until it is quite hot.

4 Carefully slide the patties into the oil and cook in the oil for about 3 minutes on each side, until golden and crisp. Remove with a slotted spatula, drain on kitchen paper and serve immediately.

> **Variation**
> For a more traditional version of bubble and squeak, heat 30ml/2 tbsp vegetable oil in a frying pan. Add 1 finely chopped onion and cook over low heat, stirring occasionally, for about 5 minutes, until softened but not coloured. Using a slotted spoon, transfer the onion to a bowl and mix with the other ingredients in step 1, omitting the cheese and using finely chopped cooked cabbage or Brussels sprouts. Use the same frying pan, with additional oil, for cooking the patties in step 4.

Bubble and Squeak

Whether you have leftovers, or cook this old-fashioned potato classic from fresh, be sure to give it a really good 'squeak' (fry) in the pan so it turns a rich honey brown as all the flavours caramelize together. It is known as colcannon in Ireland, where it is turned in chunks or sections, producing a creamy brown and white cake.

Serves 4
60ml/4 tbsp vegetable oil
1 onion, finely chopped
450g/1lb floury potatoes, cooked
   and mashed
225g/8oz cooked cabbage or
   Brussels sprouts, finely chopped
salt and ground black pepper

1 Heat 30ml/2 tbsp of the oil in a heavy frying pan. Add the onion and cook, stirring frequently, until it has softened but not browned.

2 In a large bowl, mix together the potatoes and cooked cabbage or sprouts and season with salt and plenty of ground pepper to taste. Add the vegetables to the pan with the onions, stir well, then press the mixture into a large, even cake.

4 Cook over a medium heat for about 15 minutes until the cake is browned underneath.

5 Invert a large plate over the pan, and, holding it tightly against the pan, turn them both over together. Lift off the frying pan, return it to the heat and add the remaining oil. When hot, slide the cake back into the pan, browned side up.

6 Cook over a medium heat for 10 minutes or until the underside is golden brown. Serve hot, in wedges.

> **Cook's Tip**
> If you don't have leftover cooked cabbage or Brussels sprouts, shred raw cabbage and cook in boiling salted water until tender. Drain, then chop.

Cheese Bubble and Squeak Energy 181kcal/762kJ; Protein 8.5g; Carbohydrate 21g, of which sugars 2.4g; Fat 7.7g, of which saturates 4.5g; Cholesterol 68mg; Calcium 130mg; Fibre 1.6g; Sodium 447mg.
Bubble and Squeak Energy 219kcal/908kJ; Protein 2.5g; Carbohydrate 17.2g, of which sugars 2.5g; Fat 15.9g, of which saturates 1.9g; Cholesterol 0mg; Calcium 33mg; Fibre 2.6g; Sodium 14mg.

Potato Pampushki

When these crunchy Russian potato dumplings are split open, a tasty, creamy curd cheese and chive filling is revealed.

Serves 4
225g/8oz potatoes, peeled and diced

675g/1½lb potatoes, peeled and left whole
2.5ml/½ tsp salt
75g/3oz/scant ½ cup curd cheese
30ml/2 tbsp chopped fresh chives
ground black pepper
oil, for deep frying

1 Put the diced potatoes in a large pan. Add water to cover and bring to the boil. Add salt, then simmer for about 10 minutes, or until the potatoes are tender, but do not let them get too soft. Drain thoroughly and then return to the pan and mash thoroughly. Set aside.

2 Coarsely grate the whole potatoes and squeeze out as much water as possible. Put them in a bowl with the mashed potato, salt and black pepper. Mix together. In another bowl, mix the curd cheese and chives together.

3 Using a spoon and your fingers, scoop up a portion of the potato mixture, slightly smaller than an egg, and then flatten to a circle. Put 5ml/1 tsp of the cheese filling into the middle, then fold over the edges and pinch to seal. Repeat with remaining potato and cheese mixtures, to make about 12 dumplings.

4 Heat the oil to 170°C/340°F in a heavy pan or deep-fat fryer. Deep-fry the dumplings for about 10 minutes, or until deep brown and crisp on the outide. Drain well on kitchen paper and serve immediately.

> **Cook's Tip**
> *Pampushki are traditionally cooked in stock or water and served with soup. If you prefer to poach them, add 15ml/ 1 tbsp plain (all-purpose) flour and 1 beaten egg to the mixture and poach the dumplings for 20 minutes.*

Hash Browns

Crispy golden wedges of potato, 'hashed' up with a little onion, are a favourite American breakfast dish, but they will satisfy your potato cravings and taste delicious at any time of the day.

Serves 4
450g/1lb medium potatoes
60ml/4 tbsp sunflower or olive oil
1 small onion, chopped
salt and ground black pepper
chives, to garnish
tomato sauce, to serve

1 Put the potatoes in a large pan. Add water to cover and slowly bring to the boil. Add salt, then simmer for about 15 minutes, or until the potatoes are just tender, but do be careful not let them get too soft. Drain thoroughly and leave aside to cool.

2 When cool, peel the potatoes and grate them or chop into small even chunks.

3 Heat the oil in a large heavy frying pan until very hot. Add the potatoes in a single layer. Sprinkle the onion on top and season well with salt and pepper.

4 Cook on a medium heat, pressing down on the potatoes with a spoon or spatula to squash them together.

5 When the potatoes are nicely browned underneath, turn them over in sections with a spatula and fry until the other side is also golden brown and lightly crisp, pressing them down firmly again.

6 Serve immediately with a garnish of chopped chives and tomato sauce alongside.

> **Variation**
> *Turn this side dish into a main meal by adding other ingredients to the potatoes in the pan, such as sliced (bell) peppers, tomatoes or even grilled and chopped aubergine (eggplant) for an exotic twist.*

Pampushki Energy 201kcal/852kJ; Protein 6.7g; Carbohydrate 36.6g, of which sugars 3.4g; Fat 4.4g, of which saturates 2.7g; Cholesterol 11mg; Calcium 39mg; Fibre 2.3g; Sodium 125mg.
Hash Browns Energy 183kcal/764kJ; Protein 2.1g; Carbohydrate 19.3g, of which sugars 2.3g; Fat 11.4g, of which saturates 1.4g; Cholesterol 0mg; Calcium 11mg; Fibre 1.3g; Sodium 13mg.

Potato Kugel

This traditional Jewish potato accompaniment can be prepared with butter but this recipe uses vegetable oil, which gives a much lighter, healthier result. Perfect served with roasted vegetables.

Serves 6–8
2kg/4¹/₂lb potatoes

2 eggs, lightly beaten
120–180ml/8–12 tbsp medium matzo meal
10ml/2 tsp salt
3–4 onions, grated
120ml/4fl oz/¹/₂ cup vegetable oil
ground black pepper

1 Preheat the oven to 200°C/400°F/Gas 6. Peel the potatoes and grate them finely. Place the grated potatoes in a large mixing bowl and add the beaten eggs, matzo meal, salt and ground black pepper. Mix together until thoroughly combined. Stir in the grated onions, then add 90ml/6 tbsp of the vegetable oil.

2 Pour the remaining 30ml/2 tbsp oil into an ovenproof dish that is large enough to spread the potato mixture out to a thickness of no more than 4–5cm/1½–2in. Heat the dish in the oven for about 5 minutes, or until the oil is very hot.

3 Carefully remove the dish from the oven. Spoon the potato mixture into the dish, letting the hot oil bubble up around the sides and on to the top a little. (The sizzling oil helps to crisp the kugel as it cooks.)

4 Bake the kugel in the oven for about 45–60 minutes, or until tender and golden brown and crisp on top. Serve immediately, cut into wedges.

Cook's Tip
Don't be tempted to grate the onions in the food processor as the action of the knife creates a bitter flavour by breaking down the cells of the onion flesh.

Lyonnaise Potatoes

Two simple ingredients are prepared separately and then tossed together to create the perfect combination. These potatoes go very well with a simple main course, such as grilled halloumi. Serve with a bowl of French beans, tossed in butter.

Serves 6
900g/2lb floury potatoes
vegetable oil for shallow frying
25g/1oz/2 tbsp butter
15ml/1 tbsp olive oil
2 medium onions, sliced into rings
sea salt
15ml/1 tbsp chopped fresh parsley

1 Scrub the potatoes clean and put them in a large pan. Add water to cover and bring to the boil. Add salt, then simmer for about 15 minutes, or until the potatoes are tender, but do not let them get too soft.

2 Drain the potatoes through a colander and leave to cool slightly. When the potatoes are cool enough to handle, peel and finely slice them.

3 Heat the vegetable oil in a large, heavy frying pan and shallow fry the potatoes in two batches for about 10 minutes until crisp, turning occasionally.

4 Meanwhile, melt the butter with the oil in a separate frying pan and fry the onions for 10 minutes until golden, stirring frequently. Drain the cooked onions thoroughly on pieces of kitchen paper.

5 Remove the potatoes with a slotted spoon and drain on kitchen paper. Toss with sea salt and carefully mix with the onions. Sprinkle with the parsley and serve.

Cook's Tip
Boiling the potatoes with their skins on allows them to retain their shape; this makes finely slicing them after they have been boiled far easier.

Potato Kugel Energy 361kcal/1516kJ; Protein 8g; Carbohydrate 56.2g, of which sugars 6.8g; Fat 12.8g, of which saturates 1.8g; Cholesterol 48mg; Calcium 38mg; Fibre 3.7g; Sodium 538mg.
Lyonnaise Potatoes Energy 248kcal/1037kJ; Protein 3.6g; Carbohydrate 30.7g, of which sugars 6.6g; Fat 13.2g, of which saturates 3.4g; Cholesterol 10mg; Calcium 31mg; Fibre 2.7g; Sodium 50mg.

Colombian Cheesy Potatoes

Tender new potatoes are coated in a creamy cheese and tomato sauce.

Serves 6
1kg/2¼lb new or salad potatoes
25g/1oz/2 tbsp butter
4 spring onions (scallions), sliced

2 large tomatoes, peeled, seeded and chopped
200ml/7fl oz/scant 1 cup double (heavy) cream
90g/3½oz/1 cup grated mozzarella
salt and ground black pepper

1 Place the potatoes in a large pan of salted cold water. Cover and bring to the boil, then simmer for 18–20 minutes, until tender.

2 Meanwhile, melt the butter in a frying pan, add the spring onions and cook gently for 5 minutes, until softened. Stir in the tomatoes and cook for a further 2–3 minutes, stirring occasionally, until the tomatoes break up.

3 Drain the potatoes and put them in a warmed serving bowl. Add the cream to the onion and tomato mixture, bring to the boil, then add the cheese, stirring until it melts. Season to taste. Pour the hot sauce over the potatoes and serve immediately.

Creamed Sweet Potatoes

This dish uses white sweet potatoes rather than the orange variety.

Serves 4
900g/2lb sweet potatoes

50g/2oz/¼ cup butter
45ml/3 tbsp single (light) cream
freshly grated nutmeg
15ml/1 tbsp chopped fresh chives
salt and ground black pepper

1 Peel the sweet potatoes, cut them into large chunks and place in a pan of water. Boil for 20–30 minutes until tender.

2 Drain the potatoes and return them to the pan. Add the butter, cream, nutmeg, chives and seasoning. Mash with a potato masher and serve warm.

Glazed Sweet Potatoes with Ginger and Allspice

Fried sweet potatoes acquire a candied coating when cooked with ginger, syrup and allspice. The addition of cayenne pepper cuts through the sweetness and prevents the dish from becoming cloying.

Serves 4
900g/2lb sweet potatoes
50g/2oz/¼ cup butter

45ml/3 tbsp vegetable oil
2 garlic cloves, crushed
2 pieces preserved stem ginger, drained and finely chopped
10ml/2 tsp ground allspice
15ml/1 tbsp syrup from the preserved ginger jar
salt and cayenne pepper
10ml/2 tsp chopped fresh thyme, plus a few thyme sprigs, to garnish

1 Peel the sweet potatoes and cut them into 1cm/½in cubes. Melt the butter with the oil in a large frying pan. Add the sweet potato cubes and fry, stirring frequently, for about 10 minutes, until they are just soft.

2 Stir in the garlic, chopped ginger and allspice. Cook, stirring constantly, for 5 minutes more. Stir in the preserved ginger syrup. Season with salt and a generous pinch of cayenne pepper and add the chopped thyme. Stir for 1–2 minutes more, then serve, sprinkled with thyme sprigs.

Variation
For a less sweet, unglazed version of this dish, use a 2.5cm/1in piece of fresh ginger, finely chopped, instead of the preserved ginger and omit the syrup.

Cook's Tip
Some sweet potatoes have white flesh and some have yellow. Although they taste similar, the yellow-fleshed variety look particularly colourful and attractive.

Cheesy Potatoes Energy 343kcal/1430kJ; Protein 6.6g; Carbohydrate 29g, of which sugars 4.3g; Fat 25g, of which saturates 14.5g; Cholesterol 62mg; Calcium 87mg; Fibre 2.1g; Sodium 125mg.
Creamed Sweet Potatoes Energy 310kcal/1308kJ; Protein 3.1g; Carbohydrate 48.4g, of which sugars 13.3g; Fat 13g, of which saturates 8.3g; Cholesterol 35mg; Calcium 66mg; Fibre 5.4g; Sodium 189mg.
Glazed Potatoes Energy 387kcal/1627kJ; Protein 7.2g; Carbohydrate 49.5g, of which sugars 26.1g; Fat 19.3g, of which saturates 9.8g; Cholesterol 50mg; Calcium 49mg; Fibre 3.6g; Sodium 562mg.

Orange and Maple Syrup Candied Sweet Potatoes

A true taste of America, no Thanksgiving or Christmas table is complete unless sweet potatoes are on the menu. Serve with extra orange segments to make it really special.

Serves 8

900g/2lb sweet potatoes

250ml/8 fl oz/1 cup orange juice
50ml/2fl oz/¼ cup maple syrup
5ml/1 tsp freshly grated ginger
7.5ml/1½ tsp ground cinnamon
6.5ml/1¼ tsp ground
  cardamom
7.5ml/1½ tsp salt
ground black pepper
ground cinnamon, to garnish
orange segments, to serve

1 Preheat the oven to 180°C/350°F/Gas 4. Peel and dice the potatoes. Put the chunks into a large pan. Add water to cover and bring to the boil. Add salt, then simmer for about 5–8 minutes, or until the potatoes are tender, but do not let them get too soft.

2 Meanwhile, stir all the remaining ingredients together in a large mixing bowl. Spread out on to a non-stick shallow ovenproof dish.

3 Drain the diced sweet potatoes thoroughly and sprinkle over the other ingredients in the dish.

4 Place the dish in the preheated oven and bake for about 1 hour, stirring the potatoes every 15 minutes until they are tender and well coated. Serve as a accompaniment to a main dish, with orange segments and ground cinnamon.

> **Variation**
> *Butternut squash would also work well in this recipe. Replace about half the quantity of the sweet potato with the squash and cut into similar-sized pieces. Boil with the sweet potato in the pan and cook for the same length of time in the oven, mixed together with the potato in the ovenproof dish.*

Sweet Potato Salsa

Eye-catchingly colourful and delightfully sweet, this delicious salsa makes the perfect accompaniment to hot, spicy Mexican dishes.

Serves 4

675g/1½lb sweet potatoes
juice of 1 small orange
5ml/1 tsp crushed dried
  jalapeño chillies
4 small spring onions (scallions)
juice of 1 small lime (optional)
salt

1 Peel the sweet potatoes and dice the flesh finely. Bring a pan of water to the boil. Add the sweet potato and cook for 8–10 minutes, until just soft.

2 Drain off and discard the cooking water from the sweet potato, cover the pan and put it back on the hob, having first turned off the heat. Leave the sweet potato for about 5 minutes until the excess liquid has evaporated, then transfer to a bowl and set aside to cool.

3 Mix the orange juice and crushed dried chillies in a bowl. Chop the spring onions finely and add them to the orange juice and chilli mixture.

4 When the sweet potato is cool, add the orange juice mixture and toss carefully until all the pieces are coated.

5 Cover the bowl and chill for at least 1 hour, then taste and season with salt. Stir in the lime juice if you prefer a fresher taste to the salsa.

> **Cook's Tips**
> *• This fresh and tasty salsa is very good served with simple grilled (broiled) or barbecued vegetables. It also makes a delicious accompaniment to slices of grilled halloumi.*
> *• The salsa will keep for 2–3 days in a covered bowl in the refrigerator. Leaving the salsa to stand in this way will also help the flavours to develop.*

Candied Sweet Potatoes Energy 124kcal/529kJ; Protein 1g; Carbohydrate 31.6g, of which sugars 26.1g; Fat 0.2g, of which saturates 0g; Cholesterol 0mg; Calcium 22mg; Fibre 0.9g; Sodium 461mg.
Sweet Potato Salsa Energy 153kcal/653kJ; Protein 2.4g; Carbohydrate 36.7g, of which sugars 9.9g; Fat 0.7g, of which saturates 0.2g; Cholesterol 0mg; Calcium 47mg; Fibre 4.2g; Sodium 69mg.

Bean Paste, Sweet Potato and Chestnut Candies

It is customary in Japan to offer special bean paste candies with tea. These sweet potato and chestnut candies tend to be very sweet by themselves, but contrast well with Japanese green teas; in particular, large-leaf Sencha and Bancha.

Makes 18
450g/1lb sweet potato, peeled
   and roughly chopped
1.5ml/¼ tsp salt
2 egg yolks
200g/7oz sugar
60ml/4 tbsp water
75g/5 tbsp rice flour or plain
   (all-purpose) wheat flour
5ml/1 tsp orange flower water or
   rose water (optional)
200g/7oz canned chestnuts in
   syrup, drained
caster (superfine) sugar,
   for dusting
2 strips candied angelica
10ml/2 tsp plum or
   apricot preserve
3–4 drops red food colouring

1 Place the sweet potatoes in a heavy pan, cover with cold water and add the salt. Bring to the boil and simmer until tender, about 20–25 minutes.

2 Drain well and return to the pan. Mash the sweet potatoes well, or rub through a fine strainer. Place the egg yolks, sugar and water in a small bowl, then combine the flour and orange flower or rose water (if using). Add to the purée and stir over a gentle heat to thicken for about 3–4 minutes. Turn the paste out on to a tray and cool.

3 To shape the sweet potato paste, place 10ml/2 tsp of the mixture into the centre of a wet cotton napkin. Enclose the paste in the cotton and twist into a nut shape. If the mixture sticks a litte, ensure that the fabric is kept properly wet.

4 To prepare the chestnuts, rinse away the syrup and dry well. Roll the chestnuts in caster sugar and decorate with strips of angelica. To finish the candies, colour the plum or apricot preserve with red colouring and decorate each one with a spot of colour. Serve in a Japanese lacquer box or on a plate or tray.

Mung Bean and Potato Dumplings

These sweet and savoury rice and potato dumplings are often served with jasmine tea.

Serves 6
100g/3½oz/scant ½ cup split
   mung beans, soaked for
   6 hours and drained
50g/2oz/½ cup rice flour
115g/4oz/generous ½ cup caster
   (superfine) sugar
300g/10½oz/scant 3 cups
   glutinous rice flour
1 medium potato, boiled in its
   skin, peeled and mashed
75g/3oz/6 tbsp sesame seeds
vegetable oil, for deep-frying

1 Put the mung beans in a large pan with half the caster sugar and pour in 450ml/¾ pint/scant 2 cups water. Bring to the boil, stirring constantly until all the sugar has dissolved. Reduce the heat and simmer gently for 15–20 minutes until the mung beans are soft. You may need to add more water if the beans are becoming dry, otherwise they may burn.

2 Once the mung beans are soft and all the water has been absorbed, reduce the beans to a smooth paste in a mortar and pestle, or use a blender or food processor, and set aside the paste to cool.

3 In a large bowl, beat the flours and remaining sugar into the mashed potato. Add about 200ml/7fl oz/scant 1 cup water to bind the mixture into a moist dough. Divide the dough into 24 pieces, roll each one into a small ball, then flatten with the heel of your hand to make a disc and lay out on a lightly floured board.

4 Divide the mung bean paste into 24 small portions. Place one portion of the paste in the centre of a dough disc. Fold over the edges of the dough and then shape into a ball. Repeat for the remaining dumplings.

5 Spread the sesame seeds on a plate and roll the dumplings in them until evenly coated. Heat enough oil for deep-frying in a wok or heavy pan. Fry the balls in batches until crisp and golden. Drain on kitchen paper and serve warm.

Mung Bean Dumplings Energy 321kcal/1346kJ; Protein 7g; Carbohydrate 40g, of which sugars 21g; Fat 16g, of which saturates 2g; Cholesterol 0mg; Calcium 104mg; Fibre 3.1g; Sodium 0mg.
Bean Paste Candies Energy 300kcal/1278kJ; Protein 10.5g; Carbohydrate 66.5g, of which sugars 22.1g; Fat 1g, of which saturates 0.2g; Cholesterol 0mg; Calcium 94mg; Fibre 7.8g; Sodium 24mg.

Sweet Potato, Apple and Bean Paste Cakes

A mixture of mashed sweet potato and a hint of apple is shaped into cubes, covered in batter and then seared in a hot pan to seal in the natural moisture. Aduki bean paste is also made into cakes by the same method.

Serves 3 (makes 6)
about 250g/9oz canned neri-an
   (Japanese soft aduki bean
   paste), divided into 3 pieces

For the batter
90ml/6 tbsp plain
   (all-purpose) flour
pinch of sugar
75ml/5 tbsp water

For the stuffing
150g/5oz sweet potato, peeled
¼ red eating apple, cored
   and peeled
200ml/7fl oz/scant 1 cup water
50g/2oz/¼ cup sugar
¼ lemon

1 Put all the ingredients for the batter in a bowl and mix well until smooth. Pour the batter into a large, shallow dish.

2 Dice the sweet potato and soak it in plenty of cold water for 5 minutes to remove any bitterness, then drain well.

3 Coarsely chop the apple and place in a pan. Add the water and sweet potato. Sprinkle in 7.5ml/1½ tsp sugar and cook over a moderate heat until the apple and potato are softened.

4 Add the lemon juice and remove the pan from the heat. Then drain the sweet potato and apple and crush them to a coarse paste with the remaining sugar in a bowl.

5 Using your hands, shape the mixture into three cubes.

6 Heat a non-stick frying pan. Coat a cube of mixture in batter, then, taking great care not to burn your fingers, sear each side of the cube on the hot pan until the batter has set and cooked.

7 Repeat this procedure with the remaining mixture and with the neri-an, shaped into similar-sized cubes. Arrange one of each type of cake on a small plate and serve hot or cold.

Fruit and Sweet Potato Syrup

Arrope is an old Arab recipe whose name means 'syrup'. This version of it comes from the Pyrenees. It starts as a lovely fruit compote and becomes a syrupy jam, perfect with soft bread.

Serves 10
3 firm peaches
1kg/2¼lb/5 cups sugar
3 large eating apples
finely grated rind of 1 lemon
3 firm pears
finely grated rind of 1 orange
1 small sweet potato, 150g/5oz
   prepared weight
200g/7oz butternut squash,
   peeled, prepared weight
250ml/8fl oz/1 cup dark rum
30ml/2 tbsp clear honey

1 Cut the peaches into eighths, without peeling, and place in a large flameproof casserole. Sprinkle with 15ml/1 tbsp of the sugar. Peel and core the apples and cut into 16 segments, then arrange on top of the peaches. Sprinkle with the lemon rind and 15ml/1 tbsp of the sugar. Prepare the pears in the same way, place in the casserole, then sprinkle over the orange rind, followed by 15ml/1 tbsp of the sugar.

2 Slice the sweet potato into small pieces and spread over the top, followed by the sliced squash. Sprinkle with 15ml/1 tbsp of the sugar. Cover with a plate that fits inside the rim, weight it and leave for 2–12 hours for juice to form.

3 Put the casserole over a fairly low heat and bring to a simmer. Cook for 20 minutes, stirring once or twice. Add the remaining sugar, in three or four batches, stirring to dissolve each time. Bring the mixture up to a rolling boil and boil very steadily for 45 minutes. Stir and lift off any scum.

4 Test the reduced syrup by pouring a spoonful on a plate: it should wrinkle when a spoon is pulled across it. Off the heat, stir in the rum and honey. Return the casserole to a moderate heat and cook for a further 10 minutes, stirring frequently to prevent the fruit sticking. The colour will deepen to russet brown. Remove the pan from the heat and set aside to cool. If the resulting compote is a little too stiff, stir in some more rum before serving.

Sweet Potato Paste Cakes Energy 65kcal/275kJ; Protein 1.2g; Carbohydrate 13.6g, of which sugars 3.7g; Fat 1g, of which saturates 0.3g; Cholesterol 22mg; Calcium 19mg; Fibre 1.1g; Sodium 16mg.
Syrup Energy 308kcal/1291kJ; Protein 11g; Carbohydrate 38.1g, of which sugars 28.6g; Fat 13.2g, of which saturates 2.4g; Cholesterol 9mg; Calcium 246mg; Fibre 2.4g; Sodium 69mg.

Sweet Potato and Almond Panellets

The Catalan name for these nutty festival cakes means 'little bread', but they are, in fact, much closer to marzipan, with a slightly soft centre that is produced by their secret ingredient – sweet potato. Patisserie shops make hundreds of these little cakes for All Saints' Day, 1 November, when families take flowers to the graveyards of their relatives.

Makes about 24
115g/4oz sweet potato
butter, for greasing
1 large (US extra large)
    egg, separated
225g/8oz/2 cups ground almonds
200g/7oz/1 cup caster (superfine)
    sugar, plus extra for sprinkling
finely grated rind of
    1 small lemon
7.5ml/1½ tsp vanilla extract
60ml/4 tbsp pine nuts
60ml/4 tbsp pistachio
    nuts, chopped

1 Peel and dice the sweet potato and cook it in a pan of boiling water for about 15 minutes, until soft but not falling apart. Drain well and leave to cool.

2 Preheat the oven to 200°C/400°F/Gas 6. Line one or two baking sheets with foil and grease well with butter.

3 Put the cooled sweet potato into a food processor and process to a smooth purée. Gradually work in the egg yolk, ground almonds, caster sugar, lemon rind and vanilla extract, processing to make a soft dough. Transfer the dough to a bowl, cover with clear film (plastic wrap) and chill in the refrigerator for 30 minutes.

4 Spoon walnut-size balls of dough on to the prepared baking sheets, spacing them about 2.5cm/1in apart, then flatten them out slightly.

5 Lightly beat the egg white and brush over the cookies. Sprinkle half with pine nuts, slightly less than 5ml/1 tsp each, and half with pistachio nuts. Sprinkle lightly with sugar. Bake for 10 minutes, or until lightly browned.

6 Leave to cool on the foil, then lift off with a metal spatula.

Potato and Caraway Biscuits

These savoury potato biscuits are delicious warm or cold.

Makes 30
115g/4oz/8 tbsp butter, softened

115g/4oz/1⅓ cups mashed potato
150g/5oz/1¼ cups plain
    (all-purpose) flour
2.5ml/½ tsp salt
1 egg, beaten
30ml/2 tbsp caraway seeds

1 Preheat the oven to 220°C/425°F/Gas 7. Put the butter and mashed potato in a large bowl. Sift the flour and salt into the bowl, then mix to a soft dough. Knead the dough on a lightly floured surface until smooth. Cover and chill for 30 minutes.

2 Roll out the potato dough on a lightly floured surface until 8mm/⅓in thick. Brush with beaten egg, then cut into strips 2 × 7.5cm/¾ × 3 in. Transfer to an oiled baking sheet and sprinkle with caraway seeds. Bake for 12 minutes, or until lightly browned. Transfer to a wire rack and leave to cool.

Sweet Potato Muffins with Raisins

These muffins have the great colour of sweet potatoes.

Makes 12
1 large sweet potato, cooked,
    peeled and mashed
350g/12oz/3 cups plain
    (all-purpose) flour
15ml/1 tbsp baking powder

1 egg, beaten
225g/8oz/1 cup butter, melted
250ml/8fl oz/1 cup milk
50g/2oz/scant ½ cup raisins
50g/2oz/¼ cup caster
    (superfine) sugar
salt
12 paper muffin cases
icing (confectioners') sugar, to dust

1 Preheat the oven to 220°C/425°F/Gas 7. Sift the flour and baking powder over the mashed potatoes with a pinch of salt and beat in the egg. Stir the butter and milk together and pour into the bowl. Add the raisins and sugar and mix to combine.

2 Spoon the mixture into muffin cases. Bake for 25 minutes until golden. Dust with icing sugar and serve warm.

Panellets Energy 130kcal/541kJ; Protein 3.1g; Carbohydrate 10.7g, of which sugars 9.6g; Fat 8.6g, of which saturates 0.8g; Cholesterol 8mg; Calcium 32mg; Fibre 1g; Sodium 20mg.
Caraway Biscuits Energy 51kcal/212kJ; Protein 0.8g; Carbohydrate 4.6g, of which sugars 0.1g; Fat 3.4g, of which saturates 2.1g; Cholesterol 15mg; Calcium 9mg; Fibre 0.2g; Sodium 26mg.
Sweet Potato Muffins Energy 293kcal/1227kJ; Protein 4.1g; Carbohydrate 34.2g, of which sugars 9.3g; Fat 16.5g, of which saturates 10.1g; Cholesterol 57mg; Calcium 70mg; Fibre 1.4g; Sodium 135mg.

Sweet Potato Pie

Sweet potatoes make a wonderful pie filling and are available all year round. This spicy dessert, scented with cinnamon, ginger and nutmeg, is the perfect end to a summer barbecue or will make a deliciously warming end to a decadent winter feast.

Serves 6–8

675g/1½lb sweet
  potatoes, unpeeled
170g/6oz/1 cup light
  brown sugar
2 large (US extra large)
  eggs, separated
pinch of salt
5ml/1 tsp ground cinnamon
2.5ml/½ tsp ground ginger
1.25ml/¼ tsp grated nutmeg
175ml/6fl oz/¾ cup
  whipping cream
pinch of cream of tartar
  (if needed)
23cm/9in pie shell made from
  plain pastry

1 Put the sweet potatoes in a pan of boiling water. Simmer for 20–25 minutes, until tender. Drain and let cool. When the sweet potatoes are cool enough to handle, peel them.

2 Pureé the sweet potatoes in a blender or food processor; there should be 350ml/12fl oz/1½ cups of pureé. Preheat the oven to 190°C/375°F/Gas 5.

3 Combine the pureé, sugar, egg yolks, salt and spices in a bowl. Stir well to dissolve the sugar. Add the cream and stir to mix.

4 In another bowl, completely clean and grease free, beat the egg whites until they hold a soft peak. Add the cream of tartar when the whites are frothy.

5 Stir one quarter of the whites into the potato mixture to lighten it. Fold in the remaining whites with a metal spoon or rubber spatula.

6 Pour the filling into the pie shell and spread it out evenly. Bake for about 40–45 minutes, until the filling is set and lightly golden brown and the pastry is golden. The filling will rise during baking but will fall again when the pie cools. Serve warm or at room temperature with cream or ice cream.

Sweet Potato Scones

These are scones with a difference. A sweet potato gives them a pale orange colour and they are meltingly soft in the centre, just waiting for a knob of butter.

Makes about 24

150g/5oz sweet potatoes, peeled
  and cut into large chunks
butter, for greasing
150g/5oz/1¼ cups plain
  (all-purpose) flour
20ml/4 tsp baking powder
5ml/1 tsp salt
15g/½oz/1 tbsp soft light
  brown sugar
150ml/¼ pint/⅔ cup milk
50g/2oz/4 tbsp butter or
  margarine, melted

1 Put the sweet potatoes in a large pan. Add water to cover and bring to the boil, then simmer for about 8–10 minutes, or until the potatoes are tender.

2 Drain the potatoes thoroughly and leave to cool slightly, then mash and set aside.

3 Preheat the oven to 230°C/450°F/Gas 8. Grease a baking sheet. Sift together the flour, baking powder and salt into a bowl. Mix in the sugar.

4 In a separate bowl, mix the mashed sweet potatoes with the milk and melted butter or margarine. Beat until the ingredients are well blended.

5 Add the flour to the sweet potato mixture and stir until a smooth dough forms.

6 Turn out the dough on to a lightly floured surface and knead until soft and pliable.

7 Roll or pat out the dough to a 1cm/½in thickness. Cut into rounds using a 4cm/1½in cutter.

8 Arrange the rounds on the baking sheet. Bake for about 15 minutes until risen and lightly golden. Serve warm.

Sweet Potato Pie Energy 416Kcal/1736kJ; Protein 5.3g; Carbohydrate 38.2g, of which sugars 18.6g; Fat 28g, of which saturates 16.9g; Cholesterol 114mg; Calcium 98mg; Fibre 1.9g; Sodium 360mg.
Sweet Potato Scones Energy 48kcal/200kJ; Protein 0.9g; Carbohydrate 7.1g, of which sugars 1.4g; Fat 1.9g, of which saturates 1.2g; Cholesterol 5mg; Calcium 18mg; Fibre 0.3g; Sodium 18mg.

Potato Bread with Onions

This potato bread is utterly delicious served warm with a simple vegetable soup.

Makes a 900g/2lb loaf
450g/1lb/4 cups strong white
   bread flour
5ml/1 tsp easy-blend (rapid-rise)
   dried yeast
a pinch of salt, for the dough

15g/¹⁄₂oz/1 tbsp butter
325ml/11fl oz/1¹⁄₃ cups
   warmed milk
15ml/1 tbsp olive oil
2 medium onions, sliced into rings
115g/4oz maincrop
   potatoes, grated
1 sprig rosemary, chopped
2.5ml/¹⁄₂ tsp sea salt
oil, for greasing and to serve

1 Sift the flour into a large bowl. Make a well in the centre and stir in the yeast and a pinch of salt. Rub in the butter until the mixture resembles fine breadcrumbs. Gradually pour in the milk. Incorporate the ingredients with a round-bladed knife and then bring together with your fingers.

2 Turn the dough out and knead on a floured surface until it is smooth and elastic. Return the bread to a clean bowl and cover with a damp cloth. Leave to rise in a warm place for 45 minutes or until the dough has doubled in size.

3 Meanwhile, heat the oil in a pan and add the onions, stir over a low heat and cook for about 20 minutes until the onions are golden brown and very soft. Set aside. Boil the grated potatoes in lightly salted water for 5 minutes or until just tender.

4 Turn the dough out of the bowl and knock back (punch down). Roll out on a lightly floured surface. Drain the potatoes and sprinkle half over the surface with a little rosemary and half the onions. Carefully roll the dough up into a sausage shape.

5 Lift the dough into an oiled 23 × 23cm/9 × 9in flan tin (pan). Using the palms of your hands, flatten the dough out. Sprinkle with the remaining potatoes, onions, salt and rosemary. Cover again with a damp cloth and leave to rise for 20 minutes.

6 Meanwhile, preheat the oven to 220°C/425°F/Gas 7. Bake for 15–20 minutes. Serve warm drizzled with a little oil.

Cheese and Potato Bread Twists

A complete Ploughman's lunch, with the cheese and potato cooked right in the bread. This makes an excellent base for a filling of strong Cheddar cheese.

Makes 8
225g/8oz floury
   potatoes, diced

225g/8oz/2 cups strong white
   bread flour
5ml/1 tsp easy-blend (rapid-rise)
   dried yeast
150ml/¹⁄₄ pint/²⁄₃ cup
   lukewarm water
175g/6oz/1¹⁄₂ cups red Leicester
   cheese, finely grated
10ml/2 tsp olive oil, for greasing
salt

1 Cook the potatoes in a large pan with plenty of lightly salted boiling water for 20 minutes or until tender. Drain through a colander and return to the pan. Mash until smooth and set aside to cool.

2 Meanwhile, sift the flour into a large bowl and add the yeast and a good pinch of salt. Stir in the potatoes and rub with your fingers to form a crumb consistency.

3 Make a well in the centre and pour in the water. Start by bringing the mixture together with a round-bladed knife, then use your hands. Knead for 5 minutes on a well-floured surface. Return the dough to the bowl. Cover with a damp cloth and leave to rise in a warm place for 1 hour or until doubled in size.

4 Turn the dough out and knock back the air bubbles. Knead it again for a few seconds. Divide the dough into 12 pieces and shape into rounds.

5 Sprinkle the cheese over a baking sheet. Take each ball of dough and roll it in the cheese. Roll each cheese-covered roll on a dry surface to a long sausage shape. Fold the two ends together and twist the bread. Lay the bread twists on an oiled baking sheet.

6 Cover with a damp cloth and leave the bread to rise in a warm place for 30 minutes. Preheat the oven to 220°C/425°F/Gas 7. Bake the bread for 10–15 minutes. Serve hot or cold.

Cheese Twists Energy 231kcal/971kJ; Protein 8.7g; Carbohydrate 26.4g, of which sugars 0.8g; Fat 10.4g, of which saturates 5.2g; Cholesterol 21mg; Calcium 203mg; Fibre 1.2g; Sodium 162mg.
Potato Bread Energy 2154kcal/9113kJ; Protein 61.1g; Carbohydrate 423.9g, of which sugars 52.5g; Fat 36g, of which saturates 13.9g; Cholesterol 54mg; Calcium 1154mg; Fibre 22.1g; Sodium 332mg.

German Potato Bread

This is an adaptation of the classic German-style bread. This version is made with strong white flour and floury potatoes.

Makes a 450g/1lb loaf

175g/6oz potatoes, peeled and
   cut into chunks
butter, for greasing
225g/8oz/2 cups strong white
   bread flour
10ml/2 tsp baking powder
5ml/1 tsp salt
15ml/1 tbsp vegetable oil
paprika, for dusting
mustard-flavoured butter,
   to serve

1 Put the potatoes in a large pan. Add water to cover and bring to the boil, then simmer for about 15 minutes, or until the potatoes are tender, but do not let them get too soft.

2 Drain the potatoes thoroughly in a colander and then return to the pan. Mash with a potato masher or pass through a potato ricer or food mill into the pan and set aside.

3 Preheat the oven to 230°C/450°F/Gas 8. Grease and line a 450g/1lb loaf tin (pan).

4 Sift the flour into a large bowl and mix together with baking powder and the salt.

5 Rub the mashed potato into the dry ingredients making sure you achieve an even mixture.

6 Stir in the oil and 200ml/7fl oz/scant 1 cup lukewarm water. Turn the dough into the tin and dust with the paprika.

7 Bake in the oven for 25 minutes. Turn out on to a wire rack to cool. Cut the bread into thick chunks and serve with mustard-flavoured butter.

> **Cook's Tip**
> This bread is best eaten while still warm, with lashings of the mustard-flavoured butter.

Thin Potato Bread

This is a traditional bread from Norway, known as lefse. The many types of lefse are all very thin, slightly soft potato breads. They can be eaten buttered and sprinkled with sugar or served with honey or cloudberry jam. Lefse can also be wrapped around a filling of houmous or filled with a salad.

Makes about 35

1kg/2¼lb potatoes
40g/1½oz/3 tbsp butter
120ml/4fl oz/½ cup single
   (light) cream
450–600g/1–1⅓lb/4–5 cups
   plain (all-purpose) flour
salt

1 Put the potatoes in a large pan. Add water to cover and bring to the boil, then simmer for about 15 minutes, or until the potatoes are tender, but do not let them get too soft.

2 Drain the potatoes thoroughly in a colander and then return to the pan. Mash with a potato masher or pass through a potato ricer or food mill into the pan and set aside. Add the butter, single cream and about 5ml/1 tsp of salt and beat together. Set aside to cool.

3 When the potatoes are cool enough to handle, add enough flour to form a firm dough. On a lightly floured surface, knead the dough until smooth.

4 Divide the dough into pieces about the size of a large egg, roll into balls and put on a baking tray. Chill in the refrigerator for 30 minutes.

5 On a lightly floured surface, roll out each ball of dough until very thin. Heat a large ungreased frying pan or flat griddle until hot.

6 Cook the breads in batches over a medium heat, one at a time, until brown spots appear on the upper surface. Turn them over with a metal spatula and cook the second side. Put the breads between two dish towels to stop them from drying out. Serve immediately.

German Bread Energy 989kcal/4191kJ; Protein 24.1g; Carbohydrate 203g, of which sugars 5.7g; Fat 14.4g, of which saturates 1.8g; Cholesterol 0mg; Calcium 326mg; Fibre 8.7g; Sodium 1991mg.
Thin Potato Bread Energy 71kcal/301kJ; Protein 1.8g; Carbohydrate 14.7g, of which sugars 0.6g; Fat 1g, of which saturates 0.5g; Cholesterol 2mg; Calcium 23mg; Fibre 0.7g; Sodium 5mg.

Index